Walking Victoriously Through a Fiery Furnace

*True Story of Betrayal, Falsehood
and Healing a Wounded Soul*

written & designed by
Jennifer Lynn Heck

When you pass through the waters,
I will be with you; and
when you pass through the rivers,
they will not sweep over you.
When you walk through the fire,
you will not be burned;
the flames will not set you ablaze.
For I am the LORD your God,
the Holy One of Israel, your Savior…

Isaiah 43:2-3, NIV

Walking Victoriously Through a Fiery Furnace
Copyright © 2023 by Jennifer Lynn Heck

Written & designed by Jennifer Lynn Heck, Louisville, Kentucky

Front cover illustration by Ol41ka | Shutterstock.com
Back cover illustration by Eky Studio | Shutterstock.com

Inside illustrations from Shutterstock.com | alphaspirit.it, Amanda Carden, Anastasios71, Apostrophe, Arnold.Petersen, Bruce Rolff, DarkBird, esfera, Federico Magonio, Galushko Sergey, Garsya, Grycaj, John Theodor, Khabarushka, Krivosheev Vitaly, MarinaGrigorivna, Masson, pryzmat, Rachata Sinthopachakul, selyavin, Smileus, spinspinspin, SvetaZi, TaraPatta, Tilted Hat Productions, TonTonic, Welena

Real identity of Russ on pages 78-81 is Chad Russell of Louisville, Kentucky; his testimony and quotations are used with his permission.

Photo of author on page 133 by Susan Speece
Photo of author and Rick Jarvis tandem skydiving on page 133 by Jim Bedway

All rights reserved. No part of this publication may be reproduced, distributed, or transmitted in any form or by any means, including photocopying, recording, or other electronic or mechanical methods, without the prior written permission of the author, except in the case of brief quotations embodied in critical reviews and certain other noncommercial uses permitted by copyright law. For permission requests, contact Jennifer Lynn Heck at jennifer.heck@jjjheck.com.

The Living Bible copyright © 1971 by Tyndale House Foundation. Used by permission of Tyndale House Publishers Inc., Carol Stream, Illinois 60188. All rights reserved. The Living Bible, TLB, and the The Living Bible logo are registered trademarks of Tyndale House Publishers.

Scripture quotations marked MSG are taken from THE MESSAGE, copyright © 1993, 2002, 2018 by Eugene H. Peterson. Used by permission of NavPress. All rights reserved. Represented by Tyndale House Publishers, Inc.

THE HOLY BIBLE, NEW INTERNATIONAL VERSION®, NIV® Copyright © 1973, 1978, 1984, 2011 by Biblica, Inc.® Used by permission. All rights reserved worldwide.

Scripture quotations marked NLT are taken from the Holy Bible, New Living Translation, copyright © 1996, 2004, 2015 by Tyndale House Foundation. Used by permission of Tyndale House Publishers, Inc., Carol Stream, Illinois 60188. All rights reserved.

Some content taken from *Seven Keys to Spiritual Renewal* by Stephen Arterburn and David Stoop. Copyright © 1998. Used by permission of Tyndale House Publishers. All rights reserved.

Independently Published

Printed by Amazon Kindle Direct Publishing

ISBN: 979-8-84935-173-5

First Edition

With overflowing love and gratitude,
I dedicate this book to Lord God.
Throughout my life,
he has been my faithful companion,
walking with me through intense fiery trials.

~

Lord, you alone can heal me,
you alone can save,
and my praises are for you alone.
Jeremiah 17:14, TLB

Table of Contents

PREFACE
**Sounding the Alarm on Falsehood &
Offering Healing to Wounded Souls** 9

EPISTLE
True Story of Betrayal, Falsehood and Healing 13

    Letter 1 ~ God Prepares Victoria Grace
               for Her Faith Journey 14

    Letter 2 ~ Victoria Grace Returns Home
               Exhausted and Disillusioned 20

    Letter 3 ~ Victoria Meets Damien 24

    Letter 4 ~ Damien Knocks Out Victoria
               With His One-Two Punch 29

    Letter 5 ~ God Allows Victoria Grace
               to Enter a Fiery Furnace 35

    Letter 6 ~ Final Face-to-Face Showdown
               Between Victoria and Damien 40

    Letter 7 ~ God's Spirit of Truth Exposes
               the False Teacher 44

    Letter 8 ~ Victoria Warns the Church Leaders
               About Damien 54

    Letter 9 ~ Victoria Grace Researches
               Falsehood for a Year 58

    Letter 10 ~ Great Physician Begins Healing
               Victoria's Wounded Soul 61

    Letter 11 ~ Lord God Enables Victoria to
               Completely Forgive Damien 69

Table of Contents

    Letter 12 ~ Father God Teaches
                  Victoria to Trust Again 78

    Letter 13 ~ Master Potter Unveils
                  His New Creation! 83

P.S. TO THE EPISTLE
Sharing More Truth on Falsehood and Healing 89

    Letter 14 ~ Spirit of Truth Reveals
                  the Source of Falsehood 91

    Letter 15 ~ False Teachers Can Become Cult Leaders 95

    Letter 16 ~ Gardener Pulls Up the
                  Prideful Root of Falsehood 99

    Letter 17 ~ Commander In Chief Gives a WAR
                  Strategy to Defeat Satan and Falsehood 105

    Letter 18 ~ Sovereign God Responds to People
                  Choosing to Live in Falsehood 111

    Letter 19 ~ Great Physician Leads Us
                  Through the Healing of Our Souls 115

    Letter 20 ~ Master Potter Shares the Process
                  of Molding His Clay 119

- ❖ Bible Verses to Study 122
- ❖ References 131
- ❖ Resources 132
- ❖ Author & Designer of the Book 133
- ❖ Book Endorsements & Reviews 134
- ❖ Concluding Encouragement 138

An epistle is a letter written to a person or group of people. The epistle's author has specific purposes for writing the letter:

- Comforting
- Encouraging
- Challenging
- Instructing
- Warning

~ PREFACE ~
Sounding the Alarm on Falsehood & Offering Healing to Wounded Souls

*J*ENNIFER, A JOYFUL SERVANT OF CHRIST JESUS, writes this epistle to everyone who has a willing heart to believe in LORD God. Grace, truth, love, peace and wisdom be yours in abundance from God the Father, Son and Holy Spirit.

With each tick of the clock, we are one moment closer to being ushered into eternity. Whether we enter eternity through our physical death or when Christ Jesus returns to earth in glorious majesty to conquer all evil, each of us faces the paramount importance of being ready. This reality beckons every individual to make daily decisions as if that moment is now.

The Holy Spirit guarantees forgiveness of all our sins, victory over evil, transformed earthly lives and glorious eternal life in heaven through our acceptance of Father God's gracious gift. This gift is not based on our own works. Rather, God's gift to us is his finished work of love and mercy accomplished through the sacrificial death and glorious resurrection of his Son, Jesus.

> *D*early loved friends, I had been planning to write you some thoughts about the salvation God has given us, but now I find I must write of something else instead, urging you to stoutly defend the truth that God gave once for all to his people to keep without change through the years.
>
> I say this because some godless teachers have wormed their way in among you, saying that after we become Christians we can do just as we like without fear of God's punishment. The fate of such people was written long ago, for they have turned against our only Master and Lord, Jesus Christ.
>
> ~ Jude 1:3-4, TLB

Jude, servant and half-brother of Jesus Christ, shared a turning point in his epistle. He witnessed a crisis situation within the early church that caused him tremendous grief.

Ungodly individuals secretly infiltrated the church and perverted the message of Christ. By masquerading as true apostles sent by God, they smuggled in false teaching and led believers astray by mixing error with truth. Not only did these sneaky, cunning people deny Jesus Christ as the sovereign God, but they also taught that his magnificent love and forgiveness give individuals liberty to freely indulge in immoral behavior.

Regrettably, this situation was not the only one during the first century. False apostles and deceitful teachers wormed their way into many Christian churches. Jude witnessed firsthand the devastating effects of this insidious invasion. His burden to sound the alarm compelled him to write an epistle to his brothers and sisters in the faith.

Urgency of my epistle written to you

Two thousand years later, the same despicable situation exists and continues to spread throughout the world.

I, Jennifer, also feel compelled to write an epistle to you, because of a similar crisis. It happened in the life of one of my good friends. Her name is Victoria Grace. With her permission, I am sharing her vivid, real-life journey through two years of intense trials and excruciating pain.

After enduring this period of hardship with Victoria, I definitely share a similar passion with Jude. This is my plea to you:

Stay alert! Stand firm!
Fight vigilantly for God's truth and righteousness
as you encounter the spirit of the evil one in your daily life.

What you will read in the following pages may shock you. Hopefully, it will motivate you to become like the Bereans. "And the people of Berea were more open-minded than those in Thessalonica, and they listened eagerly to Paul's message. They searched the Scriptures day after day to see if Paul and Silas were teaching the truth" (Acts 17:11, NLT).

I encourage you to do the same with my epistle. Do not merely take my word. Read the Bible to verify that what I write to you is true.

Background of this epistle

IN THE YEAR 2003, I finished writing the first draft of *Walking Victoriously Through a Fiery Furnace*. With the escalating infiltration of Satan's falsehood in the world, I sense that now is the time to publish the book.

If you are familiar with the epistles in the Bible's New Testament, you will see similarities in themes to my epistle. In no way do I believe that this epistle is divinely inspired in the same way as those in the Bible. Yet I do know, after more than 45 years of walking with LORD God, the Holy Spirit guided me throughout the entire writing and designing of this book.

Confident assurance for you

THE MESSAGE OF THIS EPISTLE is of utmost importance. Unless I completely believed this, I would not have invested many hours writing it.

In the following series of letters, you will learn slick techniques Satan uses to twist the Word of God and lead people into deception. You will also discover the consequences of and God's response to people perverting his truth and victimizing their fellow human beings.

Dear friend, this epistle is written to you, even if you have experienced a different type of trauma other than false teaching. You will discover how to not only survive, but to flourish! You will find words of comfort and encouragement. Perhaps for the first time, you will come to know the Great Physician and trust him to transform your brokenness into his blessings.

If you know LORD God through his Word and a daily personal relationship with him, then you will indeed experience a victorious life. Absolutely nothing will be able to destroy you!

*The names of the story characters in this book
are not the people's real names.*

WALKING VICTORIOUSLY THROUGH A FIERY FURNACE WALKING VICTORIOUSLY THROUGH A FIERY
ACE WALKING VICTORIOUSLY THROUGH A FIERY FURNACE WALKING VICTORIOUSLY THROUGH A F
URNACE WALKING VICTORIOUSLY THROUGH A FIERY FURNACE WALKING VICTORIOUSLY THROUG
IERY FURNACE WALKING VICTORIOUSLY THROUGH A FIERY FURNACE WALKING VICTORIOUSLY TH
GH A FIERY FURNACE WALKING VICTORIOUSLY THROUGH A FIERY FURNACE WALKING VICTORIOU
THROUGH A FIERY FURNACE WALKING VICTORIOUSLY THROUGH A FIERY FURNACE WALKING VICT
IOUSLY THROUGH A FIERY FURNACE WALKING VICTORIOUSLY THROUGH A FIERY FURNACE WALKI
ICTORIOUSLY THROUGH A FIERY FURNACE WALKING VICTORIOUSLY THROUGH A FIERY FURNACE
ING VICTORIOUSLY THROUGH A FIERY FURNACE WALKING VICTORIOUSLY THROUGH A FIERY FUR
WALKING VICTORIOUSLY THROUGH A FIERY FURNACE WALKING VICTORIOUSLY THROUGH A FIERY
ACE WALKING VICTORIOUSLY THROUGH A FIERY FURNACE WALKING VICTORIOUSLY THROUGH A F
URNACE WALKING VICTORIOUSLY THROUGH A FIERY FURNACE WALKING VICTORIOUSLY THROUG
IERY FURNACE WALKING VICTORIOUSLY THROUGH A FIERY FURNACE WALKING VICTORIOUSLY TH
GH A FIERY FURNACE WALKING VICTORIOUSLY THROUGH A FIERY FURNACE WALKING VICTORIOU
HROUGH A FIERY FURNACE WALKING VICTORIOUSLY THROUGH A FIERY FURNACE WALKING VICT
USLY THROUGH A FIERY FURNACE WALKING VICTORIOUSLY THROUGH A FIERY FURNACE WALKING
TORIOUSLY THROUGH A FIERY FURNACE WALKING VICTORIOUSLY THROUGH A FIERY FURNACE WA
IG VICTORIOUSLY THROUGH A FIERY FURNACE WALKING VICTORIOUSLY THROUGH A FIERY FURNA
ALKING VICTORIOUSLY THROUGH A FIERY FURNACE WALKING VICTORIOUSLY THROUGH A FIERY F
CE WALKING VICTORIOUSLY THROUGH A FIERY FURNACE WALKING VICTORIOUSLY THROUGH A FI
URNACE WALKING VICTORIOUSLY THROUGH A FIERY FURNACE WALKING VICTORIOUSLY THROUG

EPISTLE

True Story of Betrayal, Falsehood and Healing

~ LETTER 1 ~
God Prepares Victoria Grace for Her Faith Journey

*D*ear Friend,

When we encounter intense fiery trials of various kinds, they often seem unexpected and shocking. Yet, from Lord God's all-knowing and all-powerful vantage point, he is always preparing us for what is just around the bend in our life journeys.

This can be seen in the life of Victoria Grace. I want you to know her background and character. This knowledge is crucial for you to understand her season walking through a fiery furnace.

~ ❖ ~

Victoria Grace was born with a crippling, physical disability. Her intellectual and emotional development remained unharmed.

Over the years, several surgeries increased some mobility. However, Victoria accepted at a young age that she would need to deal with physical challenges and their impact for her entire life. If it were not for her joyful and determined spirit, she could have been consumed with bitterness and self-pity.

As early as age six years old, Victoria expressed her love for God by drawing the scene of Jesus Christ's birth, regardless of the time of year and even though it was a struggle for her to hold a crayon.

At the age of 12, she accepted Christ as her Savior. Victoria's decision was genuine—confessing and repenting of her sinful nature, asking Jesus into her heart and allowing him to begin transforming her life.

During high school and college, Lord God enabled Victoria Grace to achieve much success. Though, she recalled still having a hole in her soul that nothing on earth could fill. She realized that Jesus was continuing to knock on her heart's door.

At age 22, she asked him to be the sovereign Lord of her life. It was then that Victoria started experiencing consistent joy and purpose. She was no longer stifled by religion, but fulfilled in a daily relationship with God.

The calendar flipped to 1988—shortly after she graduated with a bachelor's degree, majoring in marketing.

"No way! I am never going back to college," Victoria adamantly responded to her sister's casual suggestion.

She definitely did not intend to pursue a master's degree. Victoria admitted lacking clear direction for her life, but believed it would not be found through additional education.

Seven years passed.

Victoria continued growing in her relationship with Jesus Christ. She experienced zest for life, as he gave her glimpses into how he wanted her to make an eternal difference.

She sensed the Lord was preparing her to embrace an entirely new direction. It would require Victoria giving up what she thought she wanted. It would mean leaving the safety of the shoreline and venturing alone into the depths of the unknown. In addition, it would mean being misunderstood by her family.

As the Bible instructs, Victoria sought the wisdom of several mature Christians and asked them to pray for God's direction in her life.

Persevering a season in the wilderness

ABSOLUTELY NOTHING HAPPENED for another year and a half. That is, nothing happened from a human perspective.

God seemed silent. Barriers at every turn.

Victoria could identify with the Old Testament prophet Jeremiah's impatience and bewilderment: "You [God] wrapped yourself in thick blankets of clouds so no prayers could get through" (Lamentations 3:44, MSG).

She continued living her life as usual. Yet her joyful attitude turned sour. She became frustrated, because she knew with everything in her that God had something else for her to do.

Victoria learned to wait and trust God, and wait some more.

"The one thing I did right during this season in the wilderness was to continue abiding in Christ," she said reflectively. "The Holy Spirit revealed to me that this was his purpose in what I considered to be a delay.

"He had to test my devotion to him. God had to strip me of the worldly crutches I had come to lean on. He had to observe that I found my total significance, security and dependence in him. He had to prepare me for the intense journey ahead, because he alone knew what it contained."

Stepping out in faith to attend Bible college

WHEN FATHER GOD OBSERVED that his period of preparation was complete, he parted the heavenly sound barrier of clouds. The Son's glorious rays shone brightly upon a new path.

After fasting and praying several weeks, Victoria attended a transforming 3-day spiritual retreat through her church. The very night it concluded, she drove to her parents' house to tell them that she discerned it was God's timing for her to step out in faith and pursue a new vocation.

"Keep in mind that my father knew nothing about the 'call' I sensed receiving from God," Victoria shared. "When I told him, Dad was so distraught that he walked out of his house and wouldn't talk to me for several days. My announcement also placed a strain on my parents' marriage for many months, because Mom fully supported me following God's direction in my life."

Victoria discovered that following LORD God involves costs—not only to herself, but also to others.

"As children, even adult children, we do need to honor and respect our earthly parents," she shared. "At the same time, after I became a child of God, my first allegiance is now to him. I love LORD God wholeheartedly. It is my desire to obey his plan above my own and above any other person's plan for my life."

Despite all the costs, Victoria applied to enter Bible college. One by one, God orchestrated the details to confirm his divine involvement.

Within nine months, she sold her everything-she-ever-dreamed-of condo, resigned a secure full-time job, and said farewell to family and friends. In the summer of 1997, she moved 260 miles away to live by herself on the Bible college's campus for the duration of her ministry training.

Victoria shared a similar passion with the apostle Paul:

> *And now I am going to Jerusalem,
> drawn there irresistibly by the Holy Spirit,
> not knowing what awaits me…But life is worth nothing
> unless I use it for doing the work assigned me by the Lord Jesus—
> the work of telling others the Good News
> about God's mighty kindness and love.*
> Acts 20:22,24, TLB

Learning lessons in the classroom of life

DURING THE NEXT TWO AND A HALF YEARS, Victoria Grace gained more than a second college degree.

"I learned as much outside the classroom," she recalled. "The Bible was not merely a textbook. It became my private tutor as the Holy Spirit showed me how it applied to my personal journey with the Lord.

"I also learned to depend even more on God. He allowed me to experience one faith trial after another. In the midst of it all, an amazing thing happened. My love for him grew by leaps and bounds."

Victoria's most severe test of endurance came during the final three weeks before graduation: eight exams, two term papers, several class projects and all of the tasks involved with moving her residence.

This season of Victoria's life resembled a marathon. Like wearing blinders, her vision remained focused straight ahead. She desired to faithfully complete this leg of her journey in a pleasing manner for her head coach, Jesus.

"Daily, and sometimes hourly, I asked the Lord to grant me sufficient strength and ability. He always provided!" said Victoria with humble gratitude.

"After completing my eighth exam and handing in the final term paper, tears of joy and thanksgiving filled my eyes and praises to the Lord filled my home-away-from-home. Jesus faithfully walked with me every step of the way!"

~ ❖ ~

BY THIS TIME, you can attest to the fact that Victoria's faith in LORD God was sincere and strong. She persevered through many challenges and trials to earn her second bachelor's degree.

She did more than merely finish—she excelled.

Victoria earned a 3.92 grade point average out of 4.0. She graduated summa cum laude.

*Little did Victoria Grace realize
that she soon would be snatched from
God's haven of refuge and headed
straight into a fiery furnace—
the intensity of which
she had never experienced!*

~ LETTER 2 ~
Victoria Grace Returns Home
Exhausted and Disillusioned

*D*ear Friend,

Victoria graduated from Bible college in December 1999. During her last night on campus, she began feeling ill and slept restlessly. By morning, she dreaded the 260-mile drive home. Her body started shutting down.

Alone in her car and struggling to concentrate, she prayed fervently. Half-jokingly and half-seriously, she asked God, "Can you please supernaturally transport me home between the two cities like you did for Philip?" *[See Acts 8:26-40]*

Upon arriving safely in her hometown five long hours later, she collapsed, shivering with chills. The next morning she awoke with a temperature of 102 degrees, severe chest congestion and body aches. A visit to the doctor was inevitable.

The prescribed antibiotic cleared up Victoria's infection within a week, but then she entered into an emotional slump. She found herself socially disconnected after living in another city for two and a half years. In addition to physical exhaustion and emotional isolation, Victoria's spiritual attentiveness to God's guidance also suffered from her weakened condition.

"In spite of what others thought I should do," she recalled, "I decided to take however long I needed to recover and savor being in the presence of my Lord before seeking employment."

Victoria's situation proved to be precarious. Her future vocation was uncertain. Prior to entering Bible college, God guided her to select a narrow field of specialized study. This choice, along with Victoria's disability, restricted her job possibilities.

Before graduating, she networked with several people. Now it was definite. The one job she desired with her whole heart slipped from her grasp. Therefore, on top of everything else, Victoria had to surrender her yearning to serve in that particular position of employment. She needed to allow Lord God to heal her disappointed heart and to lead her ever onward in his will.

Victoria cried so much that her tears could have filled a bathtub. She came to understand what King David penned:

> *You have seen me tossing and turning through the night.*
> *You have collected all my tears and preserved them in your bottle!*
> *You have recorded every one in your book.*
>
> Psalm 56:8, TLB

People associate tears mostly with sadness. Victoria's tears also contained longing of her innermost being to be in communion with the Lord, listening and obeying him.

She vividly described her spiritual hibernation through an airplane analogy. "Once I landed back home from Bible college, I hoped that the control tower [God] would give me clearance to taxi, refuel and then take off again on the next leg of my journey. Instead, I was instructed to park the plane inside the hangar.

"With heartache, yet obedience, I sat anxiously in the cockpit, fine-tuning my radio, watching other planes take off and land around me, gazing up at the bright Son shining through the control tower—longing to help passengers get to their appointed destinations."

God kept Victoria in this holding pattern for three months.

"I spent hours in intimate fellowship alone with the Lord, reading his Word, praying and singing to him. A lot of our time together was my listening in silence as the snow blanketed the world outside."

As a result, Lord God graciously renewed Victoria's body and soul through these extended conversations and times of quietness. He nourished, strengthened and comforted her as she delighted in his presence.

Sometime during this precious time, the Holy Spirit reminded Victoria of a letter she had written her father nine months earlier.

> *Dad, I know that it was practically unbearable for you to see*
> *me move far away from home. I hope by now you are able to see*
> *all the fantastic results that have occurred through it.*

If God hadn't enabled me to take the step of total surrender and faith in him, I could NEVER have grown deeper in love with him and learned more of his daily presence in my life.

Yes, it has truly been the hardest thing I have ever experienced. However, with each new demanding situation comes a greater dependence upon him to become the woman he wants me to be.

Just because I am moving back after finishing Bible college doesn't mean that my life will get easier. In fact, if I am committed to continue growing in my relationship with the Lord (which I am!), he will give me even greater challenges in which to obey and glorify him.

Little did Victoria Grace realize, as she recalled those words, that she soon would be snatched from God's haven of refuge and headed straight into a fiery furnace—the intensity of which she had never experienced!

$\mathcal{A}$ faint signal,
like a tiny blip on a radar screen,
flashed deep within Victoria.
The blip disappeared
just as quickly as it emerged.

~ LETTER 3 ~

Victoria Meets Damien

Dear Friend,

As Victoria Grace continued soaking up the glorious Son's rays of warmth and nourishment, another employment opportunity appeared on the horizon. Her family and friends agreed that it seemed to be the perfect fit for her passion, training and skills. She seized the opportunity and accepted the job.

Around the same time, Victoria ran into Lauren, a casual church friend whom she had not seen since leaving for Bible college. After some chit-chat and learning that Victoria was at a crossroads, Lauren enthusiastically concluded that Victoria would be an ideal participant for a Bible study that she attended.

When Lauren guaranteed it would take her to the next level of faith in Christ, Victoria jumped at the opportunity.

Although the Bible study was not directly affiliated with a church, the teacher's expressed desire was to recreate the early church, as recorded in the book of Acts, by unifying all believers in Christ Jesus. According to Lauren, the teacher's emphasis was on breaking racial, social and denominational barriers, sharing with each other Christ's unconditional love and living in joyful praise to creator God.

All of this appealed to Victoria. Excitement bubbled inside her. She anticipated gaining new biblical insight into God's presence and direction in her life.

Blown away on first encounter

VICTORIA WAS UNABLE TO ATTEND the first Bible study gathering. That night, torrential rain and wind swept through the city.

When she called the teacher, he seemed gracious in understanding her decision not to drive in severe weather. At the same time, he added that nothing like that ever scared him. All he needed to do was to call upon God's angels, who would calm the storm and protect him.

"Wow!" thought Victoria. "This man's faith is incredible."

She most certainly agreed that God assists his people through the ministering work of angels. Yet a faint signal—like a tiny blip on a radar screen—flashed deep within Victoria. It was not so much what the man said, but rather the tone of his voice. Was there a hint of self-endued power?

The blip disappeared just as quickly as it emerged.

Despite her phone conversation with the teacher, she remained firm in her conviction not to go to the first Bible study meeting. He accepted her decision, but asked Victoria to come early to the second gathering at his house, so he could bring her up to the level of the other group members.

Uneasiness fluttered within Victoria when she heard his request. Through past experience and biblical mentoring, she knew it was wise for men and women to guard themselves against potentially compromising situations in private settings.

Victoria kept recalling the teacher's well-known reputation for demonstrating a Christ-like character. So, she squelched her twinge of discomfort. She compromised by going to his home later than he requested, but shortly before other group members would arrive.

For several weeks, Victoria prepared herself through prayer to be focused solely on Christ. By the time she reached the man's house, her mind and heart were centered upon the Lord and what he wanted to do next with her sincere devotion to him.

Since this was the first time they met face to face, the teacher formally introduced himself with the etiquette of a gentleman. Damien was his name.

They were alone in his house for 15 minutes. To Victoria's surprise, Damien sat close to her on the sofa, closer than she expected. She scooted away a bit, all the while maintaining eye contact and listening attentively to his summary of the previous lesson.

While he spoke, Damien casually reached over and gently touched Victoria's arm. Though their conversation continued uninterrupted, Victoria instinctively pulled her arm away to nonverbally communicate that he had crossed over a line into her personal space.

Once other people arrived, Victoria forgot the initial interaction with the teacher. Her mind and heart remained focused on the only reason she was there: to deepen her love relationship with God.

Victoria was blown away by the Bible study lesson.

"I drove home that night in a daze. Everything I learned through the years as a Christian and at Bible college seemed like crumbs compared to the feast of truth and insight this teacher served. Praises of thanksgiving to God filled my car all the way home. I could barely contain my joy, because I also perceived that this man's love and devotion to Christ was deep and intimate like mine."

Victoria's joy and enthusiasm spread like wildfire during the next gathering. A strong bond quickly formed between Damien and Victoria as she effervescently shared her faith in Christ and zest for life. To her surprise, he spontaneously hugged her twice in front of the other group members.

After everyone else left, Damien and Victoria continued discussing the implications of this newfound understanding of biblical truth. He asked her to stay longer, because he said their conversation was mutually stimulating. Victoria sensed it was time to leave, because of the male-female dynamics. Though disappointed, he graciously walked her to the car.

Damien embraced her with a third tender hug. He followed it with, "I love you, Victoria."

Without hesitation, she assumed he meant loving her as a sister in Christ. Yet, as she turned to get into her car, she responded in an almost flippant tone, "Men have said before that they loved me, but they weren't sincere."

Gently placing his hand beneath her chin, Damien turned her face toward his. As soon as their eyes met, Damien softly and slowly said with much affection in his voice, "Victoria, I am VERY sincere!"

The encounter resembled a movie scene, when all the women swoon. Somehow, Victoria maintained her composure. Her legs did not go limp. Yet a fluttering stirred within her unsuspecting heart. After more chit-chat, she got into her car and drove off. In her rear-view mirror, she could see Damien standing, waving farewell.

As she opened the windows and sunroof in her car to savor the freshness of the spring night, something flew out and was carried off with the wind.

The brief—yet powerful—encounter with this man seemed to suck much wisdom out of her mind. For a second time, Victoria drove home in a daze, truly believing that Almighty God orchestrated her meeting the Bible study teacher at this specific juncture in her life.

Ironically, several weeks prior to meeting Damien, Victoria reflected upon on the following Bible verse:

*Above all else, guard your affections.
For they influence everything else in your life.*
Proverbs 4:23, TLB

Everything I learned through the years as a Christian and at Bible college seemed like crumbs compared to the feast of truth and insight this teacher served.

VICTORIA GRACE

~ LETTER 4 ~
Damien Knocks Out Victoria With His One-Two Punch

*D*ear Friend,

With each additional Bible study session, Victoria's understanding of familiar scripture passages expanded. Love and joy of Christ radiated from her even stronger. Her faith exploded as she grasped the significance that Jesus empowers all believers to live victoriously.

At the same time, she could not understand why some of the other Bible study members' enthusiasm started fading. Victoria casually made the observation to herself that the men in attendance continued to dwindle, while more women flocked to the weekly gathering. It seemed as though most men could not connect with Damien.

She shrugged it off, pondering, "Maybe women tend to be more spiritually receptive than men. Or, perhaps the men in the Bible study felt somehow threatened by Damien, because he radiates many of Christ's characteristics."

Victoria longed to continue learning and growing in her relationship with Christ. Therefore, as the Bible study progressed, she started seeking clarification from Damien on his interpretation of select passages.

He often responded vaguely and expected unquestionable acceptance, rather than stimulating inquiry. He possessed a charisma that captured his students' imaginations and created allegiance to him.

Damien's personal interest in Victoria steadily increased. Many people in the group noticed his overtly physical and verbal expressions of love to her.

"We started communicating with each other at least once a day," she recalled. "For the next several months, we were in daily contact."

Once Damien had successfully swept Victoria off her feet emotionally, he began to relate to her as his equal due to her advanced knowledge of the Bible. He appealed to her genuine hunger and thirst to grow more intimately in love with Christ Jesus.

Then, Damien threw Victoria the line that every woman longs to hear.

One morning in late spring of 2000, he called her with exhilaration in his voice. Damien quickly explained that he asked God to reveal what kind of relationship the Lord desired for him to have with her.

"Vickie, I finally know where God is leading me after a month of soul-searching," Damien blurted with a sense of excited confidence. "Last night I had an epiphany. Now, I am sure I know what God wants us to do."

By this time, Victoria's heartbeat quickened with anticipation at hearing his revelation. She remained speechless during a dramatic pause on the other end of the phone.

The silence was punctuated with Damien's tender affection. "Oh Vickie, I love you so much! In my entire life no one has ever understood me the way you do. There has never been anyone whom I can share everything—except for you."

Damien continued, "Our relationship is higher than most married couples, because we are already one in spirit and soul. I want to establish a covenant relationship with you. I want you to be my ministry partner."

Needless to say, Damien's announcement knocked Victoria clear into the stratosphere. Although she was already pretty far gone thinking rationally, God's Spirit prompted Victoria to pray for divine direction and confirmation.

The next morning she flipped on the radio and heard, "I would rather do something great for God and fail, than do nothing and succeed." The words blasted from the radio like an angelic trumpeted announcement.

Without hesitation, she became actively involved in propagating Damien's teaching. As a result, Damien and Victoria grew more intimate in sharing their thoughts, feelings and faith with each other.

> *Within one month, Damien had taken Victoria on the fastest ride of her life—from wandering in a valley to standing on a mountain peak.*

Ensnared by the promise of healing

DURING ONE OF THE BIBLE STUDY GATHERINGS, Damien's lesson digressed into a self-proclamation of his healing powers.

He shared how several years earlier he completely restored a woman's severely acne-scarred face. On that occasion, Damien said he and an eyewitness took the woman to his basement. Before he could place his hands on her face and pray, a surge of power bolted through his body and knocked the woman to the floor several feet away. The next morning, she reported having a complexion like that of a newborn baby.

Victoria sat motionless as Damien shared his firsthand experience in divine healing. After the Bible study, one of the other group members took Victoria aside. Brittany encouraged her to ask their teacher to pray for healing from her physical disability. So, she did.

"I have been waiting for you to come to me for healing," Damien said humbly. "You do realize, Vickie, that Jesus never healed people until they came to him in faith."

Victoria innocently and sincerely replied, "Damien, by now you know my deep faith. I believe that Jesus can totally heal me, if it is his will!"

Damien smiled and embraced her, as if he held a rare bird inside a locked cage. Even though he showed great satisfaction at Victoria's request, he postponed praying over her.

She found that strange.

"Let's wait until next week," said Damien. "I need time to get powered up."

It was not the first time the two of them had discussed healing. From the day they met, Damien had suggested complete bodily healing was imminent. He never showed signs of defeat when she shared at great length her past encounters with people, who harshly pointed their spiritual fingers at her for not having enough faith to be healed.

Damien continued to enthusiastically explore the limitless possibilities how Victoria could do so much more for the kingdom of God—if she would allow God's power inside her, and within Damien, to manifest itself in physical healing.

One day the following week, while they were alone together at his house, Damien indicated he was ready to pray for her healing. Victoria was ready, too. There was no barrier in her mind or heart. She expressed absolute confidence that Jesus Christ has the authority and power to heal. Victoria started envisioning herself with a perfect body and no limitations. She truly believed that she would experience immediate bodily transformation.

As they sat side by side on the sofa, with the afternoon sunlight streaming through the windows, Damien placed his right hand on her head and left hand on her crippled leg. Victoria closed her eyes, completely entrusting herself into his care. They both eagerly anticipated miraculous results.

After he concluded a surprisingly subdued prayer, she opened her eyes. There was no manifestation whatsoever of God's Spirit. Even during the prayer and laying on of his hands, no transfer of divine power occurred. Though he tried to conceal it, Damien was visibly shaken and at a loss for words about why nothing miraculous happened.

Before he could scramble to verbalize a human explanation for the divine anomaly, Victoria broke the awkward silence. Feeling compelled to say something, she acknowledged experiencing a pervading peace throughout her entire body.

A look of relief crossed Damien's face.

"Look Vickie!" he said. "Your legs are already beginning to straighten. It's only a matter of time before you will be healed. I believe you are totally healed! Soon, everyone will believe."

That was the end of it.

That is, until Victoria received a letter from Brittany, the woman who encouraged her to ask their teacher to pray for healing.

Brittany wrote:

> Victoria, I spent the morning thanking God for your healing. You are healed! We both know it is completely in His power to

do so. So, you have the faith to receive His healing. Therefore, the only question in your mind could be, "Is it His will?" Victoria, it is His will. You must believe this completely.

We know God's will from the Lord's Prayer: "Thy will be done on earth as it is in heaven." You can have heaven on earth, Victoria—even in the body!

God never intended that any of us suffer from death or disease or injury. You need to invoke His spiritual laws over the laws of this physical world—just as lowly men have overridden gravity and aerodynamics.

Can God use you now? Absolutely. He has done wonderful things through your loving heart. But, He can do all things. Think about your healing and how it will change other people. Your healing will change the entire false notions that we are at the whim of this physical world or at the whim of God's will.

"Say what?!" gasped Victoria as she read Brittany's letter. "Does Brittany really believe God's will is a whim? And, that we have power over the physical world and power over God himself?"

Whenever a person takes
the "text" out of context,
the only thing left is a CON!

~ LETTER 5 ~

God Allows Victoria Grace to Enter a Fiery Furnace

*D*ear Friend,

Like fireworks illuminating the blackest of skies, Damien bombarded the minds of his captive Bible study members with incredibly fresh new ways of understanding familiar Bible passages.

He started with truth from God's Word. As soon as he detected they were starry-eyed over his apparent higher enlightenment, he quickly interspersed more and more outlandish concepts. As fireworks explode in rapid succession, the people could no longer distinguish truth from error.

Three months into the relationship with Damien, two of Victoria's close friends noticed drastic changes in her. Neither could pinpoint the cause. Neither knew of their shared concern. Taylor and Louise started praying for God's protection over their beloved friend.

Strange as it may sound, Damien's supposed Christ-centered teaching and personal interaction were actually luring Victoria astray, rather than drawing her closer to Lord God. As a result, she started exhibiting characteristics of her human nature, rather than standing firm in her sanctification obtained through faith in Christ.

Victoria stopped all involvement with her church. Damien convinced her that she was more advanced in the faith than most people and all she needed was his Bible study. She also started criticizing the church leaders, because Damien kept saying they were placing people back under the law, instead of setting them free through God's grace. She even started wearing tight, short dresses—none of which characterized Victoria prior to meeting this man.

The gracious Lord heard and answered the daily prayers of Victoria's friends on her behalf. He turned on a divine vacuum cleaner and slowly started sucking away the dense fog that accumulated in her mind.

First, Victoria remembered something she had told Damien early in their relationship. She does not know why she said it. She told him with unwavering conviction in her voice, "If you ever deny Lord God or his Word in any way, I will leave your Bible study."

Then, the Holy Spirit brought another overlooked situation to her mind.

With trembling in her voice, she recalled, "Damien strongly encouraged us to listen to his recorded teachings repeatedly, especially when we slept. He said a part of the human brain never sleeps. Therefore, we could learn the depths of God quicker and positively change our lives forever by listening to his teachings continuously as we slept."

Victoria added, "Damien shared with us that this was the way he developed his higher spiritual understanding—listening to other people's teaching when he slept. He said that he was a modern-day prophet and his divine calling was to enlighten people to the hidden revelations within God's Word."

Although expertly disguised with false humility and unconditional love, Victoria began to see that Damien's entire belief system centered around pride and power. The following is a summary of his brainwashed theology.

- Since people are created in God's image, it means that we are all little gods and little creators.
- Due to God creating the universe through spoken words, everything is subsequently controlled by us speaking words. We possess limitless power to speak absolutely anything into existence.
- Nothing can ever harm us or result in sickness once we discover the supernatural power God created within us.
- Whenever anything or anyone opposes us, we immediately assume that we are being attacked by Satan or persecuted for our higher spiritual enlightenment.
- Every person is a spirit. We have a soul. We live in a body. Since we consist of three parts, there are three distinct salvations.
- Everyone will go to heaven, because Christ's atoning death on the cross saved everyone's spirit.

- There is no need for evangelism as it has been recognized through the ages. Instead, evangelism needs to be focused on teaching people that we are responsible for saving our own souls through unconditional love and good deeds.
- Once people learn how to save our own souls, then we will save our bodies. We will no longer be afflicted with disabilities or diseases. The power to become perfect on earth is unleashed in each individual's life by speaking Bible passages and positive affirmations repeatedly in the morning and at night.
- The goal of our faith should be to become one of the 144,000 overcomers, who are able to save our souls and bodies. Then we will be among the many saviors/deliverers who rule on God's holy mountain.
- Through the process of saving our souls and bodies, we will one day be able to look into the mirror and actually see Jesus Christ looking back at us.
- Christ will not return until the sons and daughters of God are revealed. The glory of his coming will not originate from himself, but rather through individuals who have learned how to be overcomers.
- There are seven rings around heaven. The quality and quantity of our love and deeds determine our eternal placement in one of those rings. By overcoming through saving our souls and bodies on earth, we will reach the innermost circle and reign alongside Christ on his heavenly throne.
- We do not need to wait until we get to heaven to reign with Christ. God has given us that authority right now.
- We can live in such a higher spiritual dimension of God's kingdom that we do not even need to experience physical death. We can discover how to please God to such a degree that he will take us directly to heaven, like Enoch.

Damien gave Bible verses that were supposed to prove the accuracy of his teaching. Yet he also mingled the Bible with material from other books and with other people's personal experiences, claiming divine revelation.

Dear friend, Victoria Grace discovered that disaster always lurks around the corner whenever another source of truth is considered equal, supplementary or superior to the Holy Bible.

*Whenever a person takes the "text" out of context,
the only thing left is a CON!*

Although Victoria still could not bring herself to admit the reality of the unfolding situation, her relationship with Damien started changing drastically. One day he would call her expressing sincere love and gentle concern. The next day Damien would explode with harsh accusations about her having impure motives.

On yet another day, Victoria sensed an overwhelming presence of evil and deception emanating from him. Seized by a spirit of oppression, she was gripped by the urgency to flee from his presence.

Damien demanded that Victoria love him unconditionally, while he showed no qualms about failing to reciprocate on the same holy and blameless level. She thought it odd that he continually expressed wonder at how she responded to his outbursts with mercy and grace.

It is an understatement to say that Victoria was distressed! Due to the increasingly mismatch between Damien's words and actions, God's flashing warning signals intensified for Victoria.

God burns away the dense fog with his light

Although she remained unable to regain her total equilibrium within the cyclone that she found herself engulfed, Lord Jesus graciously gave her supernatural courage.

Whenever the Holy Spirit's light of truth faintly broke through the spiritual fog, Victoria seized the moment by boldly confronting Damien's anti-Christ behavior. As the light grew stronger in penetrating the dense fog, the frequency of these confrontations increased.

Lord God continued to burn away the deception. Victoria saw many other things that had once blinded her. For example, she recalled a favorite scripture passage that she and Damien shared.

*Now to him who is able to do immeasurably more than all we ask
or imagine, according to his power that is at work within us,
to him be glory in the church and in Christ Jesus
throughout all generations, for ever and ever! Amen.*
Ephesians 3:20-21, NIV

Victoria realized that whereas she emphasized the entire passage, Damien always chose to ignore verse 21—which is a definite continuation of the preceding verse.

Consequently, Damien indirectly communicated that his focus was on the power within himself to do immeasurably more. By doing so, he willfully downplayed the passage's overall message that it is GOD's power within people, intended to bring GOD glory in Christ's church.

Taking everything into account, it was apparent that Damien deluded himself and was not able to recognize God's truth. Therefore, Victoria adopted the plan of action Jesus gave to his disciples:

Jesus Christ said, "I am sending you out like sheep among wolves. Therefore be as shrewd as snakes and as innocent as doves." ~ Matthew 10:16, NIV

~ LETTER 6 ~
FINAL FACE-TO-FACE SHOWDOWN BETWEEN VICTORIA AND DAMIEN

*D*ear Friend,

As 10 o'clock approached, darkness enveloped the living room in Damien's home. The other women had gone home from that evening's Bible study. *[By this time, all the men stopped coming.]*

Victoria and Damien were alone.

Distinct sound of crickets filled the summer night's air, along with a hoot of owls perched in the surrounding woods. An ominous atmosphere pervaded the secluded house.

The angel of the LORD encamps around those who fear him, and he delivers them.

Psalm 34:7, NIV

Victoria sat composed on the sofa beside Damien, as if she could visibly see a host of angels surrounding and shielding her.

"Damien, why did you ask me to be your ministry partner?" she bluntly asked. "And, why do you keep saying you love me so much? You told me you wanted me in your life for a long time, because there has never been anyone whom you could share everything—except for me."

He sat expressionless.

After a brief silence, Damien looked directly into Victoria's eyes and nonchalantly responded, "It was the only way I could get what I wanted out of you."

THAT WAS IT!

This brief phrase summarized both Damien's blunt confession and his despicable motives for being in relationship with Victoria—his own personal gain.

Nearly as devastating, Damien then unashamedly boasted how Brittany joined forces with him to manipulate her. Victoria could not believe her ears. Now that he had gotten everything he wanted, he did not even care that his true motives were revealed.

Damien showed no remorse.

He offered no repentance.

There was absolutely nothing that even slightly resembled being connected to the Lord and Savior Jesus Christ, whom he claimed to know and love so deeply.

Damien's uncaring words and facial expressions sent Victoria into a state of shock. Still, God most assuredly had a firm grip on her—he enabled her to retain her presence of mind and emotional control.

Just then, the phone rang.

Damien got up to answer it in the kitchen, because he said that he was expecting a call from a woman who wanted to come over that night to discuss important business.

This break gave Victoria time to catch her breath and think quickly about how to escape. She felt as if she were living a nightmare. Everything was happening so fast.

Her mind whirled and her heart raced.

In many ways, she was trapped like an insect caught in the strands of a spider's web. Alone with a devious man—in his secluded house—past twilight, Victoria realized that she was surrounded by at least ten stairs. That placed her in an even more vulnerable position, due to the limitations of her physical disability. She was totally dependent upon Damien to ensure she got down the steps safely.

She overheard him telling the caller smugly, "I'm almost done dealing with Victoria. I will call you back as soon as she leaves."

After Damien returned to his seat next to her on the sofa, Victoria initiated meaningless chit-chat to diffuse the situation. Then, she politely asked Damien for his help in walking her down the steps to the car, as he had willingly done many times before.

However, this time he gave no tender hug. It had also been Damien's custom to stand outside his back door waving as she drove off.

Not this time.

As soon as Victoria reached her car, Damien turned, walked back into his house and shut the door.

Once safely inside her car and quickly locking the doors, the reality of the dangerous situation flooded through Victoria. Tremors of fear shook her body and astonished disbelief overwhelmed her at what had just transpired.

On the 30-minute drive home, Victoria screamed against Damien and Satan. Then, she sobbed praises to God for bringing her safely out of the evil one's clutches!

*Victoria felt like a drive-thru meal
that satisfied Damien's voracious appetite.
Having consumed its value, he casually tossed
the empty bag out of the car window,
while speeding off to his next destination.*

~ LETTER 7 ~
God's Spirit of Truth Exposes the False Teacher

*D*ear Friend,

A week after Victoria's frightening face-to-face confrontation with Damien, he sent her an email—asking for her help!

By this time, she easily spotted his chameleon-like techniques. As he had done so many times before, through his endearing communication skills, Damien came across as if she was one of his few intimate confidants.

"He told me that several people within the church started questioning his teaching," Victoria said.

"Until the suspicions died down, Damien shared he planned to stop the Bible study. He also wanted to buy back all of the compact discs of his teachings from each of the participants."

He added a P.S. Here came the clincher.

"This despicable jerk actually asked me to destroy his email!" exclaimed Victoria. "Damien was attempting to eliminate all sources of damaging information to his glowing Christian reputation. Although for months he asserted what he taught was true, now he openly expressed concern about being reprimanded and censored by leaders at the church, where he had risen to a place of public popularity and widespread influence."

Victoria confessed, "I was still coming out of shock over the last traumatic five months. I now feared what Damien was capable of doing. In my overwhelming confusion, I complied with half of his request. Dumb me, I did delete his self-incriminating email from my computer and kept no hard copy.

"But, instead of having more contact with him, I threw all his teaching CDs into the garbage—exactly where they belonged. I just wanted the traumatic ordeal to be over!"

God's Spirit of truth unravels the web of falsehood

VICTORIA GRACE FELT LIKE A DRIVE-THRU MEAL that satisfied Damien's voracious appetite. Having consumed its value, he casually tossed the empty bag out of the car window, while speeding off to his next destination.

Damien possessed a mystical aura. He knew exactly the manner and duration of flirting with women—all the while he maintained his innocence. Once his female entourage satisfied his ego of being a spiritual guru, Damien cleverly withdrew from each of them and moved on to the next unsuspecting woman.

After coming out of the shock of being betrayed and used by him, Victoria moved into the next phase of her journey through the fiery furnace. The time came to squarely face reality.

She began asking herself sobering questions, trying to make sense of the previous five months. To her great heartache, she pinpointed exactly when her relationship with Damien started deteriorating.

"It all makes sense now!" Victoria recalled. "As soon as Damien got what he wanted out of me, he immediately began pulling away. He stopped giving me special attention and affection. He spoke harshly to me. He accused me of having impure motives with him."

Victoria continued, "I also remember feeling unsettled watching Damien become close friends with married women, who had money or prominence."

Damien definitely knew what he was doing when he hand-picked the participants for his Bible study. There were common traits among the women. Some were like Victoria, at vulnerable crossroads in their lives. Others suffered deep emotional scars from past personal choices or from horrid abuse inflicted upon them.

Most of the women had only a basic knowledge of the Bible. Therefore, they were easily swayed to adopt Damien's convincing interpretation of scripture passages and his liberating belief system—that people possess the ultimate power to control their own destiny.

To top it off, each woman had something of value to give Damien for his ministry or for him personally.

During the short time Victoria was involved with Damien, she witnessed some of the women buying furnishings for his house. Some introduced him to influential leaders, who had clout to endorse his teaching. Other women gave him cash and stocks. While others offered him real estate on which to build a ministry headquarters.

The result: Damien quit his job and lived off the resources of his female supporters.

More flashbacks came to Victoria's mind. She remembered the casual conversation with Lauren, the woman who first told her about Damien's life-changing Bible study. Now, Victoria realized Lauren was concerned with making a good impression on Damien by bringing him more followers.

Damien encouraged Lauren's direct involvement in his expanding ministry. He accepted expensive gifts from her. He promised to hire her as his personal assistant. Placing her total trust in him, Lauren turned in a letter of resignation at her place of employment. Only three days before her last day of work, Damien betrayed Lauren by saying it was not God's will for him to hire her. Not only that, but he also said he no longer wanted to communicate with Lauren.

When that happened, it was extremely unsettling for Victoria to observe Damien's harsh treatment of Lauren. Yet, the aura enveloping him enabled Victoria to rationalize that he would never betray her in the same way.

But, he did!

Victoria had another enlightening flashback. She remembered one evening when Brittany invited her and Damien over for a friendly dinner. Victoria now realized it was a night filled with deception and manipulation.

The first thing Victoria noticed was Brittany's house. Actually, mansion is a more accurate description. The gated driveway led to the professionally landscaped yard with two tennis courts, in-ground swimming pool and an adventurous playground for her three children.

The second thing she found odd was that Brittany's husband did not attend the dinner. When Victoria inquired of his whereabouts, Brittany avoided telling her the truth. Several days later, she found out that Brittany separated from her husband.

Was it a coincidence the marital separation occurred shortly after Brittany met Damien? The Bible vividly describes individuals like Damien:

> They must be silenced, because they are turning whole families away from the truth by their false teaching. And they do it only for money.   ~ Titus 1:11, NLT

> These are the kind of people who smooth-talk themselves into the homes of unstable and needy women and take advantage of them; women who, depressed by their sinfulness, take up with every new religious fad that calls itself "truth." They get exploited every time and never really learn.
> ~ 2 Timothy 3:6-7, MSG

Every person is born with a conscience. Listening to this internal warning system is the first line of defense for knowing right from wrong, truth from error. For a born-again believer in Christ, the second line of defense and the primary weapon of offense is found through the Holy Spirit speaking truth from the pages of the Bible.

> But the Holy Spirit tells us clearly that in the last times some in the church will turn away from Christ and become eager followers of teachers with devil-inspired ideas. These teachers will tell lies with straight faces and do it so often that their consciences won't even bother them.   ~ 1 Timothy 4:1-2, TLB

For Victoria, it was extremely disheartening and difficult to accept the reality that it is possible for individuals to become so deceived in their minds, and hardened in their hearts, that they no longer respond to the flashing signals of their conscience or to God's Word.

Upon reflection, Victoria said with certainty, "From what I experienced firsthand with Damien's mismatched words and actions, I now realized that his conscience had become deadened. It did not bother him in the least the way he treated people."

True character revealed through words and actions

Do you recall the following childhood taunt? *Sticks and stones may break my bones, but words can never hurt me.*

Whoever came up with this trite response to insensitive and cruel treatment must have either been naive or superhuman.

The words people choose to communicate with us and the words we use to interact with other people, indeed, leave an impact—either briefly or for years to come. From birth until death, it is dangerous to gloss over the effect of words. It is equally dangerous not to evaluate words in relation to the corresponding character and actions of the person speaking.

Far too often, we make snap decisions about individuals we meet and situations we encounter based solely on what our human senses detect. Some people are swayed by appearance, words or feelings. Other individuals are easily impressed by deeds, money or status.

If we fail to carefully evaluate words along with actions, we open ourselves up to allow Satan to do what he does best: deceive.

Jesus Christ, who is God clothed in humanity, taught how to avoid this trap through keen observation. He explained, "A good man produces good deeds from a good heart. And an evil man produces evil deeds from his hidden wickedness. Whatever is in the heart overflows into speech" (Luke 6:45, TLB).

By observing people's words AND actions, we discover their true character. This process takes time, interaction in varied social settings, becoming aware of warning signs and reliance on the Holy Spirit.

That is one of the many lessons Victoria learned from her experience inside the fiery furnace with Damien.

Victoria stated, "The only positive thing I can say about Damien—if you can call it positive—is that he was a superb actor. When he was in public, he radiated the characteristics of Jesus.

"However, most of the time," continued Victoria, "Damien secluded himself from the public so that people wouldn't discover his mask. For those of us whom he brought into his inner circle, it was only a matter of time before his true character seeped through his polished acting skills."

Wolves attack when sheep are vulnerable

As we have discovered in the life of Victoria Grace, there are specific circumstances that leave a person vulnerable.

In her case, she was physically exhausted from her intense training at Bible college. Victoria was also emotionally disconnected, because of living away from family and friends for two and a half years. Additionally, sadness and disappointment filled her as she accepted not being hired for what seemed to be her dream ministry job.

> *Stay alert! Watch out for your great enemy, the devil.*
> *He prowls around like a roaring lion,*
> *looking for someone to devour.*
> 1 Peter 5:8, NLT

There is no doubt that Satan's goal is to destroy the lives of God's children. The prince of this world has a definite attack plan. Satan plants seeds of confusion and deception into the minds of individuals when we are physically, emotionally and/or spiritually vulnerable.

Ponder that. Make sure you know when and where you are vulnerable. Be alert so you will not fall prey to Satan's schemes.

However, dear friend, please hear the following and let it soak deep into your mind. Whether an attack is physical, sexual, emotional or even spiritual—one time or continuous abuse—the victim should not assume responsibility for somehow causing it to happen. There is always something inside the perpetrator triggering the despicable treatment inflicted upon the victim.

Shortly after Victoria left the Bible study, one of the other women shared a perplexing situation with her. Hazel confided that she listened to Damien's teaching for five years. Although it was dynamic to hear, Hazel pondered why there was little evidence of fruit and transformation in her life.

Galatians 5:22-23 describe the fruit of the Spirit: love, joy, peace, patience, kindness, goodness, faithfulness, gentleness and self control.

Victoria also wondered, if it was indeed a higher fulfilling experience of God's truth, why did Damien's life consistently reveal a pervading emptiness, estrangement and upheaval? Where was the evidence of the Holy Spirit's presence in his life?

Jesus provided the answers to these questions:

> Beware of false teachers who come disguised as harmless sheep, but are really wolves that will tear you apart. You can detect them by the way they act, just as you can identify a tree by its fruit…Yes, the way to identify a tree or person is by the kind of fruit produced.
>
> Not all people who sound religious are really godly. They may refer to me as "Lord," but they still won't enter the Kingdom of Heaven. The decisive issue is whether they obey my Father in heaven. On judgment day many will tell me, "Lord, Lord, we prophesied in your name and cast out demons in your name and performed many miracles in your name." But I will reply, "I never knew you. Go away; the things you did were unauthorized." ~ Matthew 7:15-16,20-23, NLT

Recognizing the masquerade of deception

SOME PEOPLE CONSIDER THE BIBLE to be outdated and irrelevant to modern life. Nothing could be further from the truth. Victoria's trust in the timelessness and authenticity of the Bible skyrocketed.

The Bible clearly describes people who choose self over everything else and take advantage of others for personal gain. Victoria realized that it exposes in detail all the characteristics she discovered firsthand through her involvement with Damien.

> *But* mark this: There will be terrible times in the last days. People will be lovers of themselves, lovers of money, boastful, proud, abusive, disobedient to their parents, ungrateful, unholy, without love, unforgiving, slanderous, without self-control, brutal, not lovers of the good, treacherous, rash, conceited, lovers of pleasure rather than lovers of God—having a form of godliness but denying its power. Have nothing to do with such people.   ~ 2 Timothy 3:1-5, NIV

Stop! Please read this Bible passage again. This time, very slowly.

Jot down the characteristics of people that LORD God wants to guard you against. Let his clear warning sink deep into your mind. Then, let it guide your relationships.

The Holy Spirit brought other scripture passages alive to Victoria—passages that she thought she understood, but now leaped off the pages with monumental significance.

> *Dear* friends, do not believe every spirit, but test the spirits to see whether they are from God, because many false prophets have gone out into the world. This is how you can recognize the Spirit of God: Every spirit that acknowledges that Jesus Christ has come in the flesh is from God, but every spirit that does not acknowledge Jesus is not from God. This is the spirit of the antichrist, which you have heard is coming and even now is already in the world.   ~ 1 John 4:1-3, NIV

As Victoria recalled these verses, a light bulb clicked on inside her. Since Damien acknowledged Christ coming from God in the flesh, her guard was lowered to accept his entire teaching as truth.

She now understood what the apostle John warned in the above passage. Throughout her close involvement with Damien, there were deceptive spirits blinding her. Once she broke fellowship with him and clung tightly to Jesus, the spiritual forces of darkness no longer had a grip on her.

The apostle Paul further described the characteristics of individuals such as Damien:

> For such people are false apostles, deceitful workers, masquerading as apostles of Christ. And no wonder, for Satan himself masquerades as an angel of light. It is not surprising, then, if his servants also masquerade as servants of righteousness. Their end will be what their actions deserve.
> ~ 2 Corinthians 11:13-15, NIV

Masquerading as messengers sent by Christ.
Masquerading as servants of righteousness.
Victoria Grace finally understood the five-month entanglement with Damien. It was actually a masquerade of Satan's diabolical deception.

Jesus Christ promised,
"But when he, the Spirit of truth, comes,
he will guide you into all truth."

John 16:13, NIV

*If I remain silent,
Satan could use Damien to gain
a foothold in the church, destroying more marriages
and fraudulently using more women.
I am responsible to Almighty God
for standing up for truth and righteousness.*

VICTORIA GRACE

~ LETTER 8 ~
Victoria Warns the Church Leaders About Damien

*D*ear Friend,

In utter disgust, Victoria Grace acknowledged, "I came face to face with Satan masquerading as a highly respected Christian."

She felt overwhelmed in the necessary task of untangling falsehood from truth. Paralysis also gripped Victoria as she began coping with the destructive emotional wounds of the cold-hearted betrayal by Damien, someone she trusted.

"For several months, my thoughts and emotions were consumed with anger and bitterness," she confessed. "I screamed! I wept many times every day. I cursed Satan for his evil infiltration into Damien, who became an extremely wayward false teacher. At the same time, I wanted to pull out Damien's hair while yelling, 'How dare you treat me and other people like this!'"

Beyond all this, though, Victoria truly wanted to do something to protect other people in her church from Damien. She spent several additional months earnestly praying, seeking wisdom from a couple long-time friends and being convicted by the Bible's guidance.

The apostle Paul issued this instruction to church leaders:

> *N*ow it's up to you. Be on your toes—both for yourselves and your congregation of sheep. The Holy Spirit has put you in charge of these people—God's people they are—to guard and protect them. God himself thought they were worth dying for.
>
> I know that as soon as I'm gone, vicious wolves are going to show up and rip into this flock, men from your very own ranks twisting words so as to seduce disciples into following them instead of Jesus. So stay awake and keep up your guard....
>
> ~ Acts 20:28-31, MSG

Victoria shared honestly, "I wrestled with two plaguing questions for months: Do I remain silent in order to protect myself and my family? Or, do I speak up boldly for Christ's truth and risk potential persecution? If I still had the CDs of Damien's teachings and his self-incriminating email, my decision to speak up would be easier to make."

In all the turmoil, she forgot the Holy Spirit enabled her to request valuable information from Damien, shortly before she broke free from his Bible study. Victoria asked him for the names and mailing addresses of teachers he learned from. He gave them to her via email. She kept those emails.

She wrote the teachers for information. Two of the so-called ministries replied. One sent her a free book with its catalog. *The Third Salvation* contained EXACTLY the teachings of Damien.

"I shuddered as I read through the book," recalled Victoria. "I showed it to my good friend Louise. She said, 'This stuff is really scary and dangerous!'"

Victoria concluded, "If I remain silent, Satan could use Damien to gain a foothold in the church, destroying more marriages and fraudulently using more women. I am responsible to Almighty God for standing up for truth and righteousness."

Having drawn that crucial line in the sand, she now knew what she must do. Victoria contacted a minister at her church and requested a meeting.

Before revealing Damien's identity, she presented the evidence that she now had of his skewed teaching. After reviewing it, the minister broke the tense silence. He confirmed the teaching is definitely biblically false and extremely dangerous.

Without hesitation, he then asked Victoria, "Is Damien the man who is teaching this material?"

"Yes!" she exclaimed, feeling her huge burden smash into pieces.

Ironically, the minister told Victoria that Damien was not the only false teacher currently causing trouble amongst God's people. The church leaders were also dealing with two others at that time!

Over the previous year, they heard rumors about Damien's questionable teaching and conduct. However, the sources were unstable people and they did not provide proof. Since the minister knew Victoria's character and biblical knowledge well, he acted upon what she shared at the meeting. He presented the situation to the church Elders.

> *Warn a divisive person once, and then warn them a second time. After that, have nothing to do with them. You may be sure that such people are warped and sinful; they are self-condemned.*
> Titus 3:10-11, NIV

Although the disciplinary process seemed slow to Victoria, the church Elders faithfully executed sovereign God's prescribed guidance.

Over the next six months, they met with Damien several times. They shared God's truth with him, extended God's grace and gave him every opportunity to repent of his false teaching and ungodly behavior.

Tragically, Damien refused.

The Elders had only one option left. They expelled Damien from the church.

FALSEHOOD

~ LETTER 9 ~
Victoria Grace Researches Falsehood for a Year

*D*ear Friend,

After meeting with the church minister concerning Damien's false teaching, Victoria diligently searched the Bible for a year. She also listened to solid biblical teaching, talked with Christian leaders, and read articles and books.

"Oh yes, I desperately wanted my wounded soul to be healed as soon as possible," Victoria acknowledged. "Yet I knew that it required a decision from me. I could wallow in self-pity, let the root of bitterness grow into revenge and live the rest of my life with deep scars. Or, I could take the first step toward healing.

"In that pivotal moment, I chose to cling to God like a life preserver, because he is the author of truth. I remembered that his Word is not only my anchor, but also my compass."

Pivotal moment >> Seeking truth

THIS IS THE STARTING PLACE for anyone who genuinely desires to discover truth in every area of life. We cannot depend on our finite human intellect. We cannot trust our changing emotions. We cannot rely on our personal experiences.

Rather, we must learn to depend, trust and rely completely on the unchanging Word of God.

Through this process, Victoria feverishly pulled up one weed after another of false teaching that was planted into her mind during the five months of deception with Damien. Like never before, she realized the importance of the type of seed sown. Whether the seed is planted in a farmer's field or information entering our minds, the harvest reaped will always resemble whatever is sown.

In the case of falsehood, the reproduction process begins quickly once its seeds take root in our minds. Seemingly harmless thoughts grow into dangerous behavior, not only affecting us but also the people with whom we come in contact. Unless uprooted sprout by sprout, the wayward weeds of falsehood spread until deception consumes us.

Falsehood in any form is extremely dangerous, destructive and deadly. We cannot afford to allow its seeds to be planted into our minds in the first place.

That is why we need to take seriously the information Victoria Grace discovered along her journey of unraveling falsehood from truth. In her year-long intensive study, she recorded nine pages of Bible passages on various aspects of the one true God, falsehood and healing wounded souls. *[See pages 122-130]*

I encourage you to also read the letters in the "P.S. to the Epistle" section. They share more from Victoria's journey. Topics include:

Spirit of Truth Reveals the Source of Falsehood

~ ❖ ~

False Teachers Can Become Cult Leaders

~ ❖ ~

Gardener Pulls Up the Prideful Root of Falsehood

~ ❖ ~

Commander In Chief Gives a WAR Strategy to Defeat Satan and Falsehood

~ ❖ ~

Sovereign God Responds to People Choosing to Live in Falsehood

~ ❖ ~

Great Physician Leads Us Through the Healing of Our Souls

~ ❖ ~

Master Potter Shares the Process of Molding His Clay

Healing Wounded Souls

~ LETTER 10 ~

GREAT PHYSICIAN BEGINS HEALING VICTORIA'S WOUNDED SOUL

*D*ear Friend,

At the same time that she started her year-long study of the Bible, Satan changed his attack strategy on Victoria. He turned her poisonous emotions inward.

With her knowledge of the Bible, Victoria felt confident she would be able to detect false teaching if it ever entered her life. She now understood the apostle Paul's emphatic warning:

So be careful. If you are thinking, "Oh, I would never behave like that"
—let this be a warning to you. For you too may fall into sin.
1 Corinthians 10:12 TLB

"How could I have been so blind?" she lamented. "I felt incredibly stupid and embarrassed for falling for Damien and his teaching. I beat myself up. Shame and guilt plagued me. Worst of all, I felt like I betrayed beloved Lord Jesus—and that truly broke my heart!"

Down, down, down. Emotionally, Victoria continued in a downward sickening spiral. She wrestled with the longing for her suffering to stop.

~ ❖ ~

PEOPLE TEND TO THINK that we will not hurt as much if we move full steam ahead in life, sweeping everything negative and painful under the rug. However, we end up hurting ourselves and others even more when the pile under the rug becomes so high that we fall over it.

Regardless of what is happening in our lives, it proves beneficial to write down thoughts, feelings and insights. For believers in Christ, this activity also includes recording praises and requests, along with how God is answering prayers and working in specific areas of discipleship.

Writing in a journal is especially helpful when experiencing sorrow and suffering. Journaling allows self-expression of overwhelming pain and confusion. It helps release poisonous emotions, without harming other people as a byproduct.

~ ❖ ~

VICTORIA DECIDED TO CONTINUE THE HEALING PROCESS by uncovering the rug. She transparently shared her thoughts and feelings with LORD God.

The following are some entries from her journal during her trauma and healing in the fiery furnace.

- Never in my life have I experienced such an intense battle. Like a pulverized boxer, I am beaten down to the mat. Satan stands over me, eclipsing the light of God's truth. Glaringly, the evil one gloats as he starts counting my knockout. I can faintly hear the constant encouragement of my faithful coach, Jesus. He is beckoning me to get back up and finish the fight.

- I don't blame you, God. Isaiah 55:8-9 assures me that your thoughts are higher than my thoughts and your ways are higher than my ways. I must continue believing you are God! I must trust you!

- I am finding out how long it takes to go through the different stages of grief and healing. When I have absolutely no strength of my own left, I am learning not to despair. Lord, this is exactly where you want me—totally dependent upon you, every second of every minute.

- Sometimes the pain feels so intense that all I can do is cry. There seems to be no tears left.

- God, your Word says, "The very day I call for help, the tide of battle turns. My enemies flee! This one thing I know: God is for me!" (Psalm 56:9, TLB).

- Someone once said, "Satan trembles when he sees the weakest saint on his knees." Lord, I know that prayer confounds Satan's destructive plans.

- ◆ I am praying throughout the day, and during the night when compelled by the Holy Spirit. Saturating my mind with Bible passages. Singing praise songs in the car and at home. Being still. Listening. Waiting. Trusting. Obeying.
- ◆ Father God, if it is not time for me to die, then I need for you to teach me to trust again.

Human fatigue from fighting the battle chipped away Victoria's confidence in God healing her wounded soul. Yet, she knew that God is sovereign, creating each person inside the womb and numbering all our days (Psalm 139).

The Lord has a purpose for every moment he breathes life into us. A primary purpose is to love him with all of our heart, soul, mind and strength (Mark 12:30). Out of that intimate love relationship flows two other dominating purposes: to glorify God and to be conformed into the likeness of his Son Jesus (Isaiah 43:7, Romans 8:28-30).

Victoria still could not shake the feeling of hopelessness. She recorded in her journal, "How can I possibly glorify God when my emotions are still holding me captive?"

Healing a wounded soul is a process

HEALING IS A PROCESS—whether it is physical, emotional or spiritual healing. Although we usually do not recognize what is happening, our healing involves many stages.

The deeper the wound, or the more life-threatening, the longer it takes to completely heal. Additionally, healing of any wound always occurs from the inside out.

What is a person's soul? The mind, will and emotions.

Through her journey in the fiery furnace, Victoria gleaned this wisdom and discovered the keys that unlock the ultimate power of healing. First, immediately contact LORD God, the Great Physician. Second, follow his prescribed treatment revealed in the Bible. Third, remain in his loving care to receive his one-on-one constant attention.

Dear friend, all of these discoveries in the healing process are not shared in this epistle merely to tell the intriguing story of Victoria Grace. They are shared as a gift to you. May you, too, come to experience the liberating freedom offered by the Great Physician to completely heal your own wounded soul.

~ ❖ ~

Just as Victoria had to walk—not run—through the fiery furnace of Satan's deception, she continued facing the reality that she must walk—not skip—through necessary stages of the healing process from being betrayed by Damien.

The more Victoria cried out to Lord God, the Great Physician, for healing and insight, the more transparent she became in acknowledging her areas of vulnerability.

"Prior to meeting Damien," Victoria pondered, "the apostle Peter and I could have been fraternal twins. Before each of our crises and turning points, we both shared a sincere devotion to Jesus. Yet we were both impulsive.

"I can now see that I became caught up in the charisma and euphoria generated by Damien. I didn't compare all of the scripture passages Damien taught against the Bible's context. I didn't allow enough time to pass before knowing his true character. And, when I first started having suspicions, I didn't seek counsel from several trustworthy advisors as discussed in the Bible."

Victoria continued, "I graduated from Bible college with honors. I knew the Bible. And I was deeply in love with Christ! Yet I fell, because I impulsively entered into a close relationship with Damien primarily based on circumstances—instead of relying on the Holy Spirit speaking to me through the combination of the Bible, prayer, other Christians AND circumstances.

"In other words, I blew it in that respect!" Victoria frankly confessed. "I accept responsibility for taking my eyes off Jesus for one tiny moment."

Although Victoria never completely abandoned Jesus—her First Love, she wept bitterly because she acknowledged momentarily turning away from God's truth. That was the same response by Peter, upon realizing his own impulsive betrayal of Lord Jesus. *[See Mark 14:66-72]*

One of Satan's strongholds is to keep reminding individuals of our failures. That is how he attacked Victoria for several months.

Yet she continually submitted to Father God's sovereign grip on her life. Victoria realized that she is indeed a vulnerable lamb and Lord God tenderly cares for her as the Good Shepherd.

When she acknowledged her part in faltering in the Christian faith and asked the heavenly Father for forgiveness, her shame and guilt were immediately removed by his marvelous grace.

> *Be careful—watch out for attacks from Satan, your great enemy. He prowls around like a hungry, roaring lion, looking for some victim to tear apart. Stand firm when he attacks. Trust the Lord; and remember that other Christians all around the world are going through these sufferings too.*
>
> *After you have suffered a little while, our God, who is full of kindness through Christ, will give you his eternal glory. He personally will come and pick you up, and set you firmly in place, and make you stronger than ever. To him be all power over all things, forever and ever. Amen.* ~ 1 Peter 5:8-11, TLB

Months passed in Victoria Grace's healing journey.

One year came and went. The calendar flipped into a second year.

With each new day, she experienced the Great Physician graciously healing her wounded soul.

Victoria honestly admitted, though, that she still had moments when the pain and injustice of her encounter with Damien seemed to eclipse God's power to transform them for his glory and purposes.

On one such occasion of fleeting doubt, the Holy Spirit prompted Victoria to ponder the biblical account of three young believers who faced a similar crisis. They had to choose to either abandon their faith in the living God and worship false gods OR stand firm for what they knew to be true and be thrown into an actual fiery furnace. They chose the latter. *[See Daniel 3:1-28]*

*The fire hadn't so much as touched the three men—
not a hair singed, not a scorch mark on their clothes,
not even the smell of fire on them!*
Daniel 3:27, MSG

As Victoria read this powerful story of invincible faith and divine deliverance, she saw similarities to her own journey.

"There is absolutely no doubt in my mind and heart," she shared. "In the midst of my journey through the fiery furnace with Satan and Damien, Lord Jesus faithfully walked beside me and rescued me like he did with Shadrach, Meshach and Abednego."

Victoria said triumphantly, "Instead of destroying me, the furnace's flames securely welded me to my beloved Lord!"

In the third chapter of Malachi in the Bible's Old Testament, Lord God explains that sometimes he uses fiery furnace trials as a refining process for our character—like removing impurities from silver and gold, which makes the metals stronger.

Victoria experienced tremendous comfort and peace being reminded that Christ Jesus always walks with her inside the fiery furnaces of life, and he is in perfect control of the intensity and duration of her painful trials.

She found herself overjoyed by all of these glorious realizations, as she reflected upon God's magnificent and intimate care for his children. Her entire perspective changed regarding the last several years of her life. With the enlightenment of the Holy Spirit, she embraced the tragedies as part of God's divine plan to refine and strengthen her faith and character.

Dear friend, when you feel the heat of the fire, remember that God has his eyes on you, holds you in the palm of his hand and walks with you through all kinds of painful and difficult trials. You are safe and secure!

*When God permits His children
to go through the furnace,
He keeps His eye on the clock and
His hand on the thermostat.*

WARREN WIERSBE

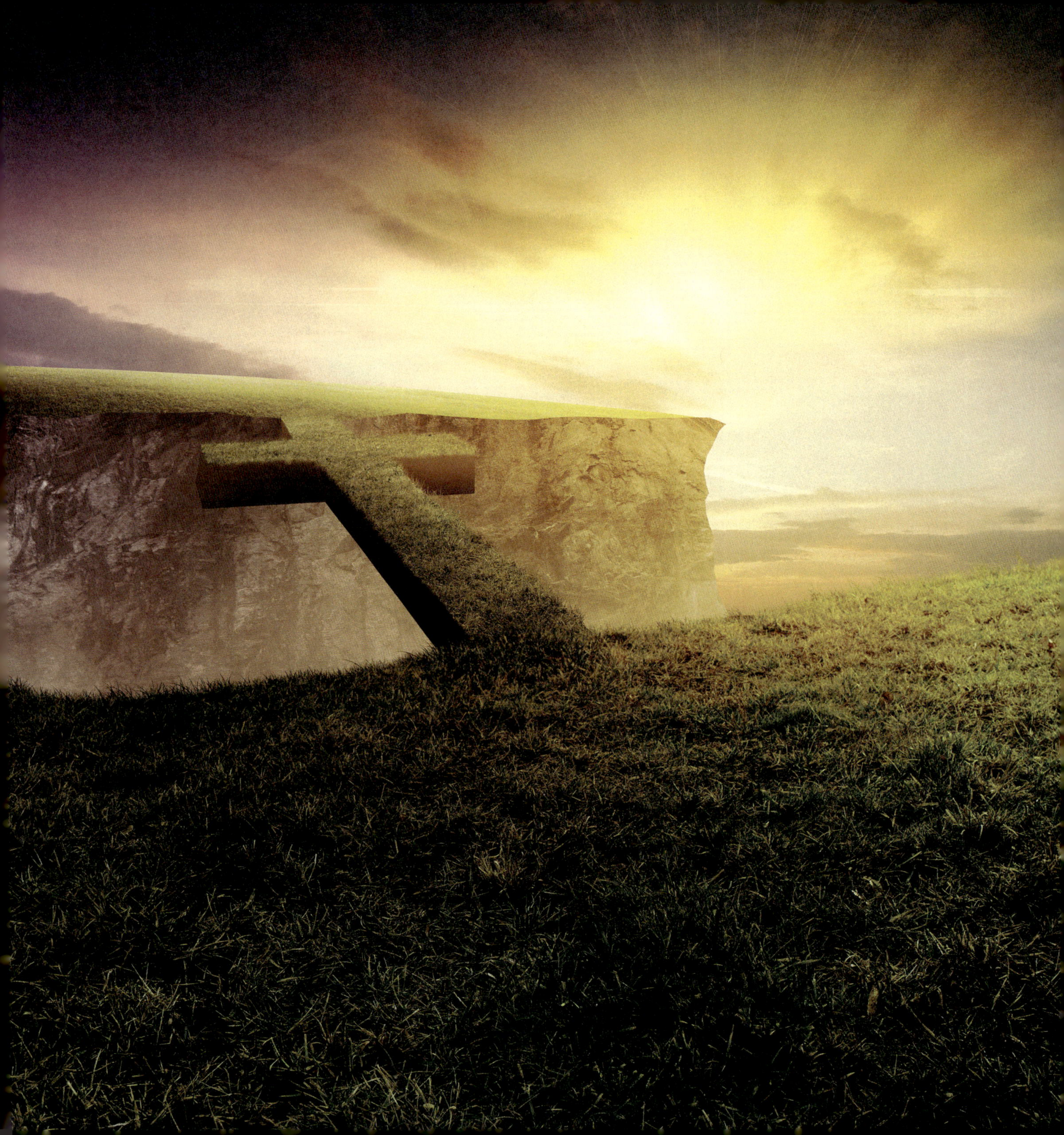

~ LETTER 11 ~
Lord God Enables Victoria to Completely Forgive Damien

Dear Friend,

Although Victoria Grace experienced much healing, God's higher purposes for this season of trials in her life had not been fully accomplished. Almighty God—the refiner and purifier of people's souls—knew that her wounded soul was not yet totally healed.

Although tempted by Satan to do so, Victoria never sought revenge for what the false teacher did to her.

The power she had to restrain herself was the Holy Spirit's assurance that the Bible is God's trustworthy Word. Deuteronomy 32:35 and Hebrews 10:30-31 promise that Lord God will execute the appropriate punishment in his divine way, at his appointed time.

No longer did Victoria focus on receiving justice for what Damien had done. Rather, she expressed more and more gratitude to Christ Jesus for sacrificing his life to forgive all her sins and to give her a new life in his kingdom.

As Victoria honestly prayed, her righteous anger toward Damien vanished.

The reality of God's love and grace only becomes life-changing when we personally encounter him.

Inside her house one wintry night, the Holy Spirit drew Victoria into the living room. Over the years, it became her private sanctuary for intimate worship and conversation with the Lord. She flipped on the spotlight over the fireplace. It illuminated the dark and silent room.

Standing in front of the mantle, Victoria's gaze fixed on a ceramic scene of Jesus Christ's physical entry into the world. Inside the humble stable, small fragile figurines of a donkey and cow looked in wonderment at Joseph, Mary and the newborn babe Jesus.

The spotlight drew her eyes upward. Victoria was overwhelmed by what she saw. Stepping backward and sitting down on the sofa, she viewed the larger scene. Above the serene depiction of Christ's birth, she saw her cherished wooden cross hanging on the wall.

It is two feet tall with a thorny wreath hanging from the top. The wreath symbolizes Christ's suffering with a crown of thorns smashed into his head. Three clusters of white dogwood flowers are stuck into the wreath, signifying purity and holiness belonging to the three persons of the Godhead.

With the cross overshadowing the nativity, Victoria's entire being absorbed the preciousness of the unfolding scene. The Holy Spirit reminded her that the cross is always part of Christ's birth, because it represents the purpose for which Jesus was born.

Victoria pondered the magnitude of how God expressed his immeasurable love for her—and for all humanity—by coming to earth. The Holy Spirit reminded her how the Bible describes in detail the horrendous, self-sacrifice Jesus willingly experienced in order to save individuals from the penalty of sin.

> *Jesus,* God in human flesh, endured unimaginable suffering and sorrow. He carried people's burdens and infirmities. He was crushed in his spirit over sin belonging to the entire world.
>
> Christ was despised and condemned by religious leaders, misunderstood by family and forsaken by friends. He was harassed, mocked, shunned and spit upon. Jesus was flogged and beaten by hate-filled men's fists. He was repeatedly struck on his head with a staff. He was blindfolded and stripped.
>
> A crown of thorns smashed into his head. Nails hammered through his hands and feet. A spear pierced his side.

"Just as there were many who were appalled at him—his appearance was so disfigured beyond that of any human being and his form marred beyond human likeness" (Isaiah 52:14, NIV).

Jesus Christ—the perfect Son of God and the only sinless human being—died an unjust, cruel and agonizing death in the presence of grief-stricken family, devastated friends, indifferent crowds and vengeful religious leaders.

Amazingly, "He never sinned, never told a lie, never answered back when insulted; when he suffered he did not threaten to get even; he left his case in the hands of God who always judges fairly" (1 Peter 2:22-23, TLB).

As Victoria reflected upon all of this, she fell to her knees and wept uncontrollably. An hour passed being encapsulated in the gripping presence of Lord God.

She lifted her bowed head and gazed upon the cross above through her blurry, teary vision. Victoria could utter only three words, "Why, my Lord?"

Hebrews 12:2 reveals the answer. This scripture says that for the JOY set before him, Christ endured the cross.

Hear that!

Jesus did not focus on the pain and suffering unjustly inflicted upon him. All that mattered to him was the joy of restoring the broken relationship between humanity and God. Christ endured the cross all out of unconditional love.

Being set free through forgiveness

Following her powerfully intimate encounter with Christ Jesus, Victoria penned the following prayer.

> Precious Lord Jesus,
> It is only because of your great love for me that I am able to come into your presence. Through your love and blood poured out on the cross, you established the new covenant with me: forgiving ALL my sins, removing ALL my guilt, restoring me to fellowship with you and giving me access into your kingdom.
> Ah Lord God, I praise your name for all of your blessings. More than for what you give me, I praise you for who you are!
> You are the creator of this universe; the maker of everything known and unknown to me. You fashioned planets and you

fashioned me inside the womb. You are my sustainer, provider, redeemer, counselor, heavenly father and friend. You are good, faithful, just, mighty, pure, holy, merciful, compassionate, and full of grace, peace, joy and loving-kindness. Lord God Almighty, you are the living Word; you are truth!

My heart is now prepared to express my prayers to you. Although I may not be able to communicate everything in words, I know that the Holy Spirit translates for me to you, Lord Jesus, and you intercede directly to Father God on my behalf.

You said, "Love your enemies and pray for those who persecute you…" (Matthew 5:44). You said, "Do not take revenge, my friends, but leave room for God's wrath, for it is written: 'It is mine to avenge; I will repay.' …Do not be overcome by evil, but overcome evil with good" (Romans 12:19,21).

My savior and master, please help me to follow your ways and to have your compassionate heart. Protect me from Satan, the evil one, and from giving into my human ways of responding to Damien.

Oh dear Lord, this man thinks he is wise. In reality, he is fooling himself. Your Word says in Galatians 6:7, "Do not be deceived: God cannot be mocked. A man reaps what he sows."

Please enlighten Damien and his followers, so they will not continue in their destructive ways. May they humble themselves before it is too late. If they really understood how it grieves you for your church body to be ripped apart—and if they really understood the damage they are doing to their souls—they would repent immediately and walk in the newness of life.

I love you wholeheartedly, Lord Jesus! You know my heart, because you know everything.

Please help me to always live like I truly believe that you live inside of me. Help me to conquer Satan's schemes with your truth and righteousness. I want your humility, loving-kindness, glory and resurrected power to radiate from me—spreading your light of unfailing hope to people in the dark and dying world. Amen!

The sheer magnitude of who God is, and what Jesus Christ willingly endured for the sake of humanity, washed over Victoria—like continuous waves lapping against the shoreline. Then, what seemed like a tidal wave crashed into her.

As she encountered Jesus, who is the only source of true forgiveness, the Holy Spirit convicted her. Victoria realized that she needed to forgive Damien.

"When you realize how much you've been forgiven, it becomes easier to forgive those who have sinned against you," explained Bob Russell and Rusty Russell in *Jesus: Lord of Your Personality*.

> *Forgiveness is a command by God.*
> *There is no exception.*

If that sounds radical, it is radical. If it sounds impossible to do, it is impossible on our own. If it sounds unfair not taking into account degrees by which someone sinned against us, it is unfair—until we realize that God does not take into account degrees of sin we commit.

Overwhelmed at the unfathomable love, mercy and grace of Lord God, Victoria wrote in her journal, "Once again, I am reminded of the significance that I must completely forgive everyone who sins against me. I now choose to forgive Damien!"

She prayed for him nearly every day and every night for an entire year. Victoria then went one step further. She wrote and mailed a letter to Damien. That may not be advisable in every person's situation. For Victoria, though, the Holy Spirit clearly led her over a nine-month period of fervent prayer to personally reach out to her perpetrator.

She biblically and boldly confronted Damien with his false doctrine and anti-Christ behavior. As she continued writing the letter, the Holy Spirit reminded Victoria of something the false teacher once shared with her.

Damien told Victoria that, when he was a child, he attended an extremely legalistic church. As a young adult, after throwing off the religious shackles enslaving him, he admitted to willfully living in total rebellion to the heavenly Father. Damien compared himself to the prodigal son as Jesus described in Luke 15:11-32.

With this understanding of his past, the Holy Spirit guided Victoria to conclude her five-page letter to him in this way:

> Damien, the Bible proclaims in Genesis 50:20, "You planned evil against me, but God used those same plans for my good and rescuing many people."
>
> God's grace is greater than what you did to me and greater than my own pain. Therefore, I choose to extend life to you through forgiveness in God's amazing grace.
>
> Father God waits for you at the crossroads. His eyes filled with loving-kindness. His arms holding a brilliant white robe, a gold ring and sandals. His longing heart gently whispers, "Come back home, Damien. You are my son. I love you!"

Victoria never heard from the false teacher.

In spite of everything, she continued praying for Damien and for his soul. She prayed that it is not too late for him to stop rebelling once again. She also prayed that he will humbly ask for forgiveness and restoration, and start walking in exhilarating newness of life with God the Father, Son and Holy Spirit.

With every fiber of her being, Victoria knows that she faithfully obeyed everything the Lord asked her to do—meeting with the church leadership to expose Damien's dangerous teaching and behavior, completely forgiving him and extending God's grace to him.

> *Now the Lord is the Spirit,*
> *and where the Spirit of the Lord is, there is freedom.*
> 2 Corinthians 3:17, NIV

Clarifying forgiveness

IN THE BOOK *SEVEN KEYS TO SPIRITUAL RENEWAL*, Stephen Arterburn and David Stoop answered the important question: "What forgiveness is NOT?" Below is their summary to guide our encounters with this often misunderstood area of Christianity.

- **Forgiveness is not condoning the behavior.** To forgive is not saying, "What you did is OK." It is saying, "The consequences of your behavior belong to God, not to me."

- **Forgiveness is not forgetting what happened.** It would be foolish to erase from mind some of the wrongs done to us. If we were to do so, we would never learn from our experiences and would walk right back into the same or a similar situation, only to face the same disappointments.

- **Forgiveness is not restoring trust in the person.** Trust is earned. It is something we give to those who deserve it. To blindly trust someone who has hurt us is naive and irresponsible.

- **Forgiveness is not agreeing to reconcile.** Reconciliation requires forgiveness, but forgiveness can be done without reconciling. It is silly, if not dangerous, to press for reconciliation when the other person is unrepentant, unchanging or unwilling.

- **Forgiveness is not doing the person a favor.** Jesus raised the standard of forgiveness to a higher level. According to him, we are to forgive even those who remain unrepentant. Forgiveness benefits the giver at least as much as it does the receiver, so we extend it whether or not the person asks for it.

- **Forgiveness is not easy.** Forgiving is difficult enough when it involves a one-time transgression. It verges on the impossible when the offense is ongoing. Such circumstances require an attitude of forgiveness, not simply an act of forgiveness.

It is absolutely vital to grasp the significance of forgiveness. If not dealt with, unforgiveness will consume our lives like an infected wound spreads poison throughout our bodies. The process of forgiving everyone who has injured us is as crucial as having emergency surgery.

With that serious urgency in mind, Arterburn shared key components of forgiveness.

- ◆ Forgiveness **IS** turning to God the Holy Spirit, asking Him to do in you what you have no power to do.
- ◆ Forgiveness **IS** choosing to move forward, beyond how a person sinned against you.
- ◆ Forgiveness **IS** no longer dwelling on your emotions of anger, bitterness, revenge, etc.
- ◆ Forgiveness **IS** releasing the person to God the Father and trusting His way of judgment.
- ◆ Forgiveness **IS** praying for the person to repent and respond to God the Son's mercy before it is too late.

What were the other results of Victoria Grace spending hours in the presence of beloved Lord Jesus?

"If the Great Physician had not done major surgery on my wounded soul," she honestly expressed, "I would have been consumed with bitterness. It would have held me hostage, as a prisoner, for the rest of my earthly life. Now that Jesus has set me free through forgiveness, he is enabling me to move forward and teaching me how to serve as a conduit of his grace to other people."

Forgiveness is a command by God. There is no exception. If it sounds unfair not taking into account degrees by which someone sinned against us, it is unfair—until we realize that God does not take into account degrees of sin we commit.

~ LETTER 12 ~
FATHER GOD TEACHES VICTORIA TO TRUST AGAIN

*D*ear Friend,

Do you recall when Victoria penned the following in her journal? "Father God, if it is not time for me to die, then I need for you to teach me to trust again."

She cried out this agonizing prayer after isolating herself from most people, for fear of being hurt and used again.

God heard her transparent prayer.

One year passed.

During that span of time, he was in the process of answering her anguish-filled plea by working simultaneously in the life of a young man. His name was Russ.

In the fullness of his time, God orchestrated events so that Victoria's friend, Jerry, invited Russ to a worship service that they attended. *It just so happened* that all three of them were grouped together for a focused time of prayer.

"As Russ briefly shared with us what God was currently doing in his life," recalled Victoria, "I sensed the powerful presence of Jesus Christ radiating from him."

With the enthusiasm of a child and the confidence of a man, Russ boldly declared that four months earlier he was born again into God's kingdom. He responded to the heavenly Father's invitation to come to him for the forgiveness of his sins. By turning toward God and away from his self-centered desires, Russ received glorious eternal life through Jesus Christ. That, in turn, completely transformed his earthly life.

After the worship service concluded, Russ shared more of his testimony with Victoria and Jerry.

Russ thought he was living right by attending church every week and being an overall good guy. Yet his life was plagued with a pattern of superficial relationships, excessive drinking, sexual immorality, earning more money and seeking social status.

Through a series of what he called *touches of God*, Russ finally realized that he had not been living the good life. He came to hate Satan as the father of all lies for blinding his mind to the light of God's truth.

After one of his encounters with the living God, Russ said, "For the first time in my life, for some reason, I prayed to the Holy Spirit. I don't know why, but I remember saying, 'Holy Spirit, please give me the strength to say what I need to say.'"

At that moment, his mouth opened and Russ said, "I want a relationship with Jesus Christ!"

Immediately, Russ experienced what he described as being full.

"That's the only way to describe what I was experiencing. Like an empty pitcher being filled with water."

Soon after professing Christ as his Lord and Savior, Russ was baptized through immersion before the church congregation. [*This public declaration of faith also demonstrates a personal turning point—choosing to die to our sins, burying our old lives in a watery grave, and God raising us to live new lives forever in Jesus Christ.*]

After being blinded by Satan for years, Russ rejoiced in Christ's light illuminating his understanding.

"I don't think you truly see how lost you were until you're found," Russ shared. "I was in church my entire life and thought God graded on the curve. Yet I was on a path to hell and had no idea. I now realize that I was lied to for 28 years by the father of lies."

Russ boldly said, "I feel betrayed. I am now at spiritual war with him, battling everyday. Satan may win some battles, but he CANNOT win the war. The war was won on the day Christ's innocent, perfect blood was shed and He was nailed to a cross and died for our sins."

Russ then shared with Jerry and Victoria his spiritual journey after accepting Christ Jesus as his Savior and Lord.

"My vision has changed completely," he said. "The Holy Spirit is giving me the ability to see the world through the eyes of what Christ would have me become. When things get blurry it's not Him, it is me. Being a Christian is not a 9 to 5 job or just giving Christ the parts of my life I want Him to have. I wrestle with it regularly, letting go and letting Him be Lord of my life."

Russ concluded by confidently and joyfully saying, "My earthly life is not mine anymore. I gave my life to Christ to be my King. I now know the only way to an eternal future in heaven is through Christ Jesus!"

As Victoria drove home after hearing that powerful testimony of Christ's transforming power, she wept and praised sovereign God.

The Holy Spirit brought Russ to Victoria's mind every day to pray for him. She realized the tremendous privilege and importance of interceding on behalf of others along their faith journeys.

Applying lessons learned inside the fiery furnace

During the next several months, Victoria and Russ started emailing and getting together for short visits. She applied the lessons she painfully learned with Damien. She carefully watched to see whether Russ's actions matched the words he professed to live by from the Bible.

Taking into account everything that she discovered through her purposeful evaluation, Victoria and Russ developed a Christ-centered friendship.

Through observing his spiritual fervor, Lord God beckoned Victoria to a renewed level of freshness, joy and hope in her own daily relationship with himself.

Something else happened through the interaction with her new friend.

Think back for a moment about what prompted Victoria to pray in agony, a year earlier, for God to take her to her heavenly dwelling. The bottom line was that she feared interacting with people because of mistrust. The deep wounds inflicted upon her by Damien resulted in Victoria shutting down emotionally and isolating herself.

"I kept seeing the brilliant light of God's truth shining forth from Russ," expressed Victoria. "That light started drawing me out from my cocoon of darkness. The more I got to know Russ, the warmth of Christ's light encouraged me to trust people again."

She confessed, "It was more than trusting people. It was relearning to completely entrust myself into the care of Father God. I realized, yet once again, that he is indeed able to protect me in relationships with people, while at the same time using them for his divine purposes."

Who would have thought that a 4-month-old Christian could have such a dramatic impact on a 24-year veteran of the faith? Who could have imagined?

The answer is simple, yet incredibly awesome: Lord God Almighty! He is, indeed, sovereign. God brings particular individuals into our lives and places us in situations at specific times to accomplish his purposes—both in our personal lives and in the world around us.

Victoria pondered the tremendous power and intimacy of God in allowing her path to cross with Russ at the particularly crucial juncture in the healing of her wounded soul.

In the spiritual realm, a fierce battle had been going on for Victoria's life, her joy and her purpose for remaining on earth. In his perfect wisdom and timing, God sent Russ as his catalyst to set her feet back firmly on his solid rock.

He also used Russ to release Victoria from her protective cocoon, which she now realized was a vital phase in the Great Physician's determined healing process. She echoed the psalmist's confident praise of assurance.

> *In my distress I prayed to the Lord,*
> *and the Lord answered me and set me free.*
> Psalm 118:5, NLT

It can certainly be seen in Victoria's new life, manifested through her transformed emotions—like the metamorphosis of a caterpillar into a butterfly.

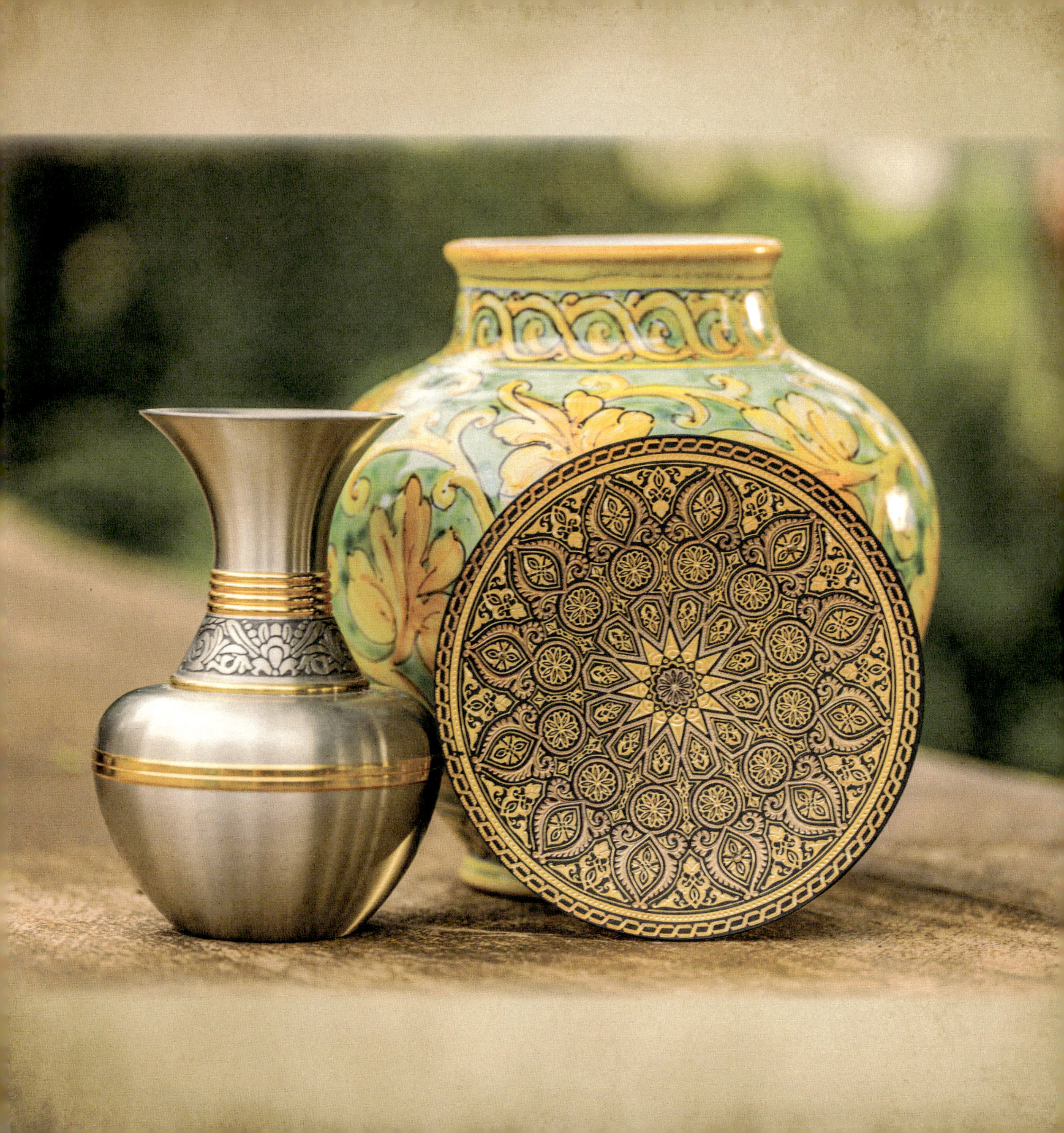

~ LETTER 13 ~

Master Potter Unveils His New Creation!

*D*ear Friend,

As Victoria Grace reflected upon the long journey of severe testing of her faith and wonderful healing of her wounded soul, she clearly recognized Lord God telling her:

> *V*ictoria, Victoria, Satan has asked to sift all of you as wheat. But I have prayed for you, Victoria, that your faith may not fail. And when you have turned back, strengthen your brothers and sisters *(based on Luke 22:31-32).*

"I now understand that God allowed me—for his divine, kingdom purposes—to be seduced by Satan through false teaching and cold-heartedly betrayed by someone I trusted," said Victoria confidently. "Out of my pain and intense trial, I developed a deeper capacity to encourage and help other people heal from their own traumas."

Victoria said with a conquering smile, "My wounded soul has been healed to such a degree that there is no longer any trace of scars! My joy and purpose in life have finally returned. However, I will NEVER be the same Victoria who people once knew!"

Do you recall how she identified herself as the spiritual twin of Peter, the apostle and close companion of Jesus Christ? After experiencing many excruciating trials of his own, Peter concluded in his first epistle that suffering is of greater worth than precious gold refined by fire.

After watching Victoria experience many painful trials and hardships through the years, I asked her a penetrating question: "Vickie, why haven't you just given up on God?"

She simply pointed me to the following Bible passage.

> *At* this point many of his disciples turned away and deserted him. Then Jesus turned to the Twelve and asked, "Are you going too?"
>
> Simon Peter replied, "Master, to whom shall we go? You alone have the words that give eternal life, and we believe them and know you are the holy Son of God."   ~ John 6:66-69, TLB

Then, Victoria shared with me this intimate reflection, "It is absolutely amazing that after being a disciple of Christ Jesus for many years, my relationship with him continues to grow more intimate and sweeter. At the same time, I recognize that I am indeed a dumb little sheep, who is vulnerable in forgetting the way to his safe and lush, green pastures."

Victoria continued, "In acknowledging my need for constant dependence upon the gentle Chief Shepherd, I realize I cannot survive a moment without his love, provision, protection, guidance and truth. It is like needing air to survive.

"Many times I am drawn to my knees in praise of who Lord God Almighty is and in thanksgiving of who I am in relation to him, one of his precious children."

Like a video playing in fast-forward mode, Victoria recalled once again her traumatic journey through the fiery furnace with Damien, the false teacher. Tears trickled down her face—no longer due to excruciating pain, but rather overwhelming gratitude. Yes, gratitude!

She recalled God's Spirit speaking the following precious words to her receptive heart.

> *My* beloved child, I have been with you every moment of your life—in your sorrows and in your joys. I have always held you securely in the palm of my hand and close to my heart.
>
> All the trials you have endured and will endure come so that my purposes will be accomplished, so that your character will be refined into the likeness of Christ, and so that you can choose to glorify me.

> Remember all of this as you live your life today and in the future. Whenever you lose sight of it, just run back into my open arms and I will lovingly show you my ways yet once again.

Receiving a unique, new name from the one true God

Dear friend, our journey walking through the fiery furnace is nearly finished. As I shared in the preface of this book, Victoria Grace is not the real name of the woman in this epistle.

Think for a moment: Have you ever considered why God changed the names of some people in the Bible? He changed Abram's name to Abraham and Sarai to Sarah. Jacob became Israel. Jesus changed Simon's name to Peter. Saul received the new identity of Paul.

Each one of these ordinary individuals experienced a powerful encounter with the one true God. He also chose them to be participants in his extraordinary plan of bringing eternal salvation to people throughout the world.

The incredible news is that this special event is not limited to individuals in the Bible. Read with great anticipation what Lord God promises those of us who believe in him:

> Let everyone who can hear, listen to what the Spirit is saying to the churches: Every one who is victorious shall eat of the hidden manna, the secret nourishment from heaven; and I will give to each a white stone, and on the stone will be engraved a new name that no one else knows except the one receiving it.
>
> ~ Revelation 2:17, TLB

In reading the background of this passage (verses 14-16), we discover that Christ Jesus fiercely denounces false teaching and promises to fight against those engaged in it if they do not repent. However, for those who remain faithful to Lord God and to his Word, he promises to give us rewards—among them will be a special new name.

This reality can be seen in Victoria's life. Like I said, Victoria Grace is not the real name of the woman in this epistle.

As I started writing this book, the Holy Spirit impressed upon me to use the name *Victoria Grace* because of what the two words beautifully illustrate. It is simple, yet profound.

*T*he only way any of us can live
victoriously in this earthly life and in eternal life
is through Lord God Almighty's glorious grace!

Our victory comes directly from what God graciously gives us through Christ Jesus. "How we thank God for all of this! It is he who makes us victorious through Jesus Christ our Lord!" (1 Corinthians 15:57, TLB).

God's grace is his unfathomable favor and blessing that we can never earn and will never deserve. His great love, forgiveness and grace gives us the victorious capacity to thrive in life and extend love, forgiveness and grace to other people.

Ponder God's magnificent grace!

I opened this series of letters to you with the urgent words of Jude. As I close my epistle, it seems appropriate to share his concluding confident proclamation. I separated the phrases with bullets to guide you in savoring the magnificent promises contained within Jude's final two verses. *[See next page]*

Dear friend, please do not skim over or hurry through this Bible passage. Let each word linger in your mind and heart—building into a crescendo of praise and adoration to God the Father, Son and Holy Spirit!

I, Jennifer, conclude this epistle by fervently praying that you will choose to live *victoriously* through God's magnificent *grace*.

Joyfully in Christ Jesus,

Jennifer

JUDE 1:24-25

- Now all glory to God,
- who is able to keep you from falling away
- and will bring you with great joy
- into his glorious presence
- without a single fault.
- All glory to him
- who alone is God, our Savior through Jesus Christ our Lord.
- All glory, majesty, power, and authority are his before all time,
- and in the present,
- and beyond all time! Amen.

Walking Victoriously Through a Fiery Furnace

P.S. to the Epistle

Sharing More Truth on Falsehood and Healing

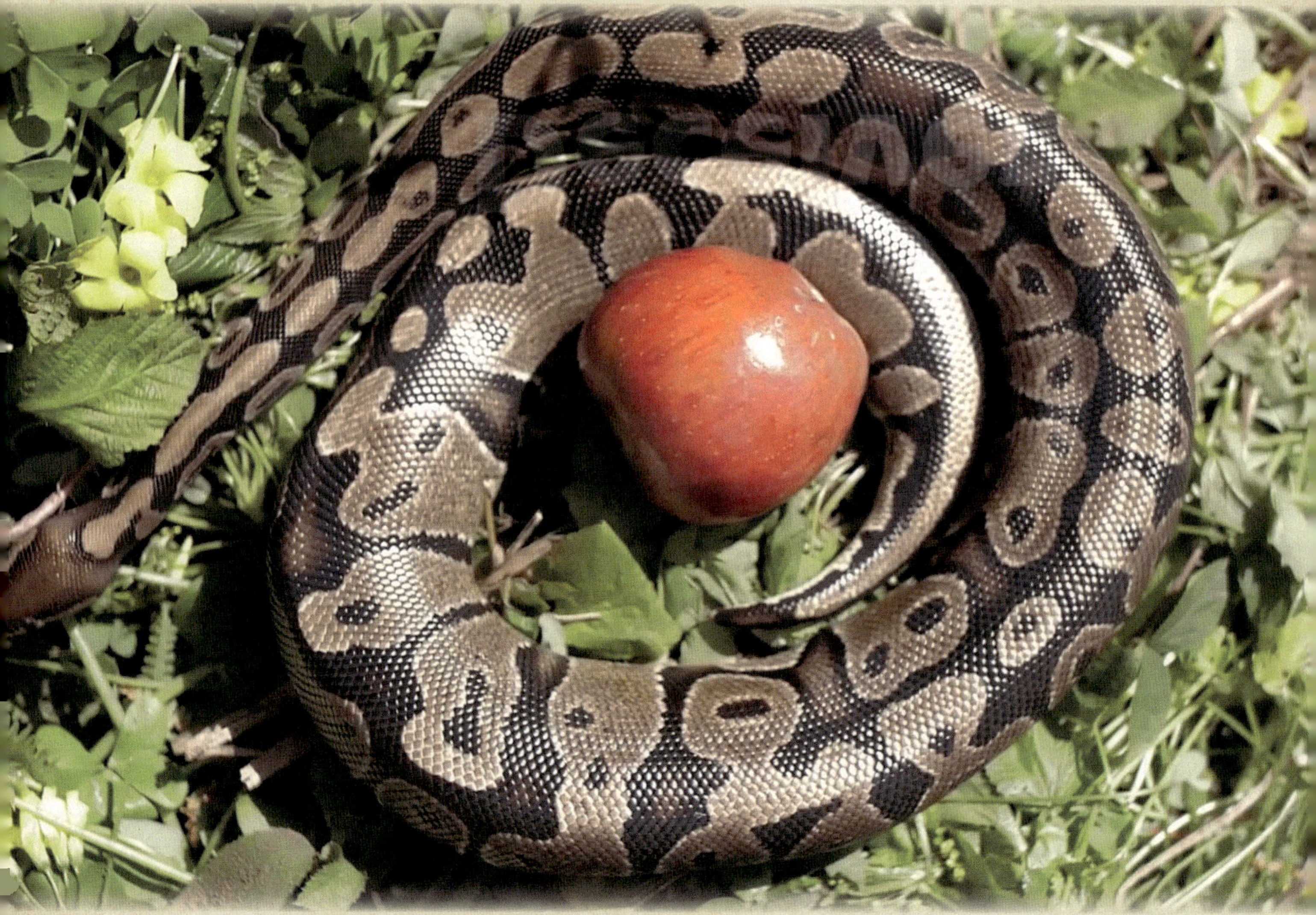

~ LETTER 14 ~
SPIRIT OF TRUTH REVEALS THE SOURCE OF FALSEHOOD

*D*ear Friend,

It is imperative to understand that not all false teachers manifest every characteristic described in the Bible. In addition, not every one of these individuals promote their wayward beliefs for the sole intent of lustfully engaging in a host of self-centered, sinful activities.

Rather, their false teaching could be the byproduct of pride, traumatic personal experiences and/or lack of sound Bible knowledge.

So, what is the ultimate origin of falsehood?

The Bible describes Satan as one of the glorious angels created by God. Yet he rebelled against the creator of the universe. Satan could no longer dwell in heaven with holy God, because in the pride of his heart he attempted to become equal with God (Isaiah 14:12-15).

Some of the other angels—now demons—followed Satan's wayward choice. They also sinned, resulting in falling from their positions of goodness and authority (2 Peter 2:4, Jude 1:6).

Ever since he was cast from the kingdom of God, Satan's mission has been to deceive and destroy humanity. He roams the earth blinding the minds of individuals to the truth and enslaving them to all kinds of evil acts. He is relentless, even though he knows God already has determined his destiny of everlasting torment in hell (Revelation 20:7-10).

Before God executes his final judgment and wrath, Satan plans to destroy everyone he possibly can and in every conceivable way.

Like a tornado, Satan leaves utter devastation in his path.

Satan is a murderer, the father of all lies and the master deceiver. Other titles he has earned through the centuries include: serpent, god of this age, enemy, devil, prince of this world, accuser, dragon, ruler of the kingdom of the air, tempter, captor, ruler of the demons, roaring lion, executioner of death, evil one, schemer, masquerader of light, leader of evil angels and the spirit at work in those who are disobedient.

Satan, the prince of the world's system, uses the same line of thought on people that he and his evil angels chose to embrace. The apostle John captures it well when he penned: "For everything in the world—the lust of the flesh, the lust of the eyes, and the pride of life—comes not from the Father but from the world" (1 John 2:16, NIV).

> Satan brings destruction and death into the world. He reverses the righteous values of nations. He creates discrimination and strife within cities. He stirs up division among church denominations and within congregations. He sneaks into the minds and hearts of individuals, whenever they ignore Lord God or choose to gratify their fleshly nature.

The evil one tries to pridefully convince people they are their own god because no other god exists. If this delusion fails, he proceeds to unashamedly trick individuals into believing there is more than one god. If Satan succeeds, then people insist there is more than one way to get to heaven besides God's way, which is only through faith in his son Jesus Christ.

Thankfully, millions of people escape Satan's snares and discover the one true God. Once we do, some tend to believe that Satan no longer has reason to bother us. Although his tactics change once individuals place our faith in Jesus, Satan's primary goal remains the same: distract, deceive and destroy.

The evil one distracts Christians, in every way possible, from maintaining our vital connection with the Savior. Satan knows if he can keep us from an intimate relationship with Christ, his evil influence over us remains unbroken.

Satan, the ruthless thief, tries to steal from every Christian. He wants to rob us of our love, trust, confidence, joy and hope in God. The evil one tells us things that are untrue about God, ourselves and other people.

The devil counterfeits everything in God's kingdom. He even plants counterfeit Christians among true believers. Satan uses the infiltration of false teachers to spread counterfeit salvation and righteousness, achieved through human effort. In addition, these individuals twist Bible passages to create divisions, confusion, fear and doubt.

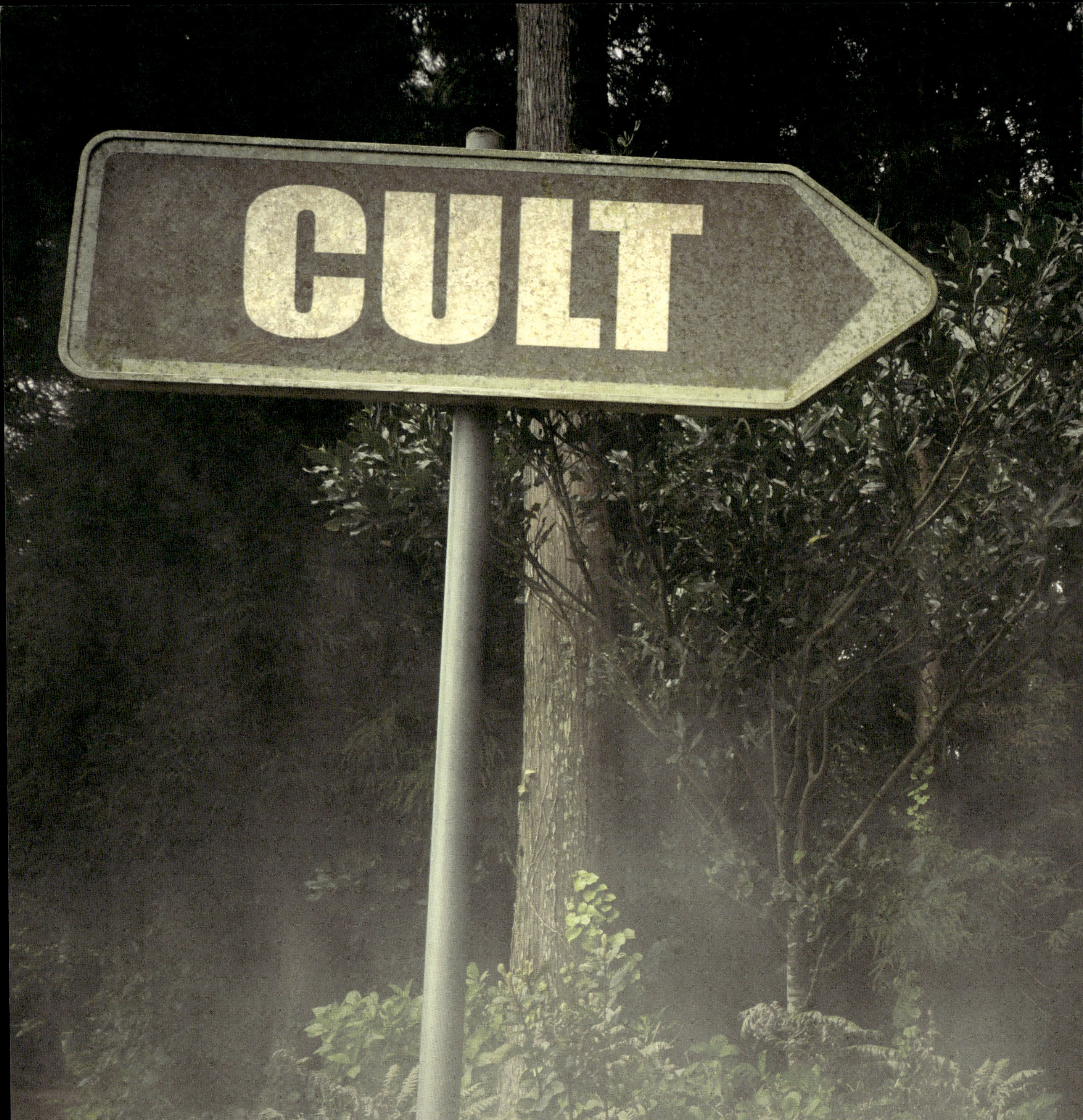
CULT

~ LETTER 15 ~
False Teachers Can Become Cult Leaders

Dear Friend,

During her year-long quest of untangling falsehood from truth, Victoria Grace acquired the following knowledge on cults.

Up until this point in her journey, she could not bring herself to articulate what she came to suspect about Damien. Victoria could now admit that he possessed many traits of a cult leader.

The apostle Paul warned first century Christians:

> *You* seem so gullible: you believe whatever anyone tells you even if he is preaching about another Jesus than the one we preach, or a different spirit than the Holy Spirit you received, or shows you a different way to be saved. You swallow it all.
> ~ 2 Corinthians 11:4, TLB

Two thousand years later, neither can we afford to be gullible and ignorant of this dangerous snare. Not all false teaching leads to the formation of cults. However, we need to know the warning signs of this insidious invasion.

"One expert on cults who grew up in a cultic group once expressed this problem to me in these terms," stated Dr. David Reagan, founder of Lamb & Lion Ministries, "Christians convert pagans. Cults convert Christians."

Terminology proves to be of utmost importance when identifying cults and responding to their members. This is according to Dr. Walter Martin, who prior to his death spent nearly 40 years researching, teaching and evangelizing in the field of cult apologetics. His comprehensive and scholastic book, *The Kingdom of the Cults*, is considered to be the definitive work.

Martin alerted Christians that cults liberally use Bible verses—almost always out of context—and evangelical clichés and terms. Cults do this purposely to convince individuals that they are Christians, too.

A cult is a religious group that masquerades as being Christian. It employs Christian terms, quotes the Bible, and uses Christian symbols. But it is not a true expression of the Christian faith.
~ Dr. David Reagan

In an article titled "The Deception of the Cults," Reagan provided an overview of the history, characteristics and dangers of cults. Besides sharing warning signs, he mentioned specific doctrinal teachings of cults that contradict God's Word. These include:

- Salvation by works
- Reincarnation
- Sexual permissiveness
- Anglo-Saxons are the true Jews
- Baptizing deceased individuals
- Denying the reality of evil, disease, death and hell
- Believing in universalism that teaches all people experience ultimate salvation

"Equally incredible," wrote Reagan, "is the cultic doctrine that is being taught on Christian television today which holds that those who are born again are 'little gods.' This is the lie that Satan told Eve in the Garden of Eden, and it is the same lie that is taught by many cultic groups."

Reagan summarized other characteristics shared by cults. He said there is usually a dynamic, charismatic founder or leader who considers himself to be either the true Christ or the last prophet of God. These false teachers use extra-biblical writings that are considered equal or superior to the Bible.

Cult leaders destroy people's confidence in the Bible and point out flaws in Christian churches. Eventually, they become the central authority in their followers' lives, assuming the place of God.

In addition, each cult views itself as God's only true church and refuses to have anything to do with any other group. The authoritarian groups are dictatorial. Someone at the top, either an individual or a collective leadership, calls all the shots.

Cult leaders pick their victims carefully because of specific vulnerabilities, promising them love, healing and provision of daily needs. They possess a mysterious power that captivates people. Once entrapped, followers are fed endless lies. They are controlled by guilt, fear and often sexual favors.

Leaders of cults isolate their followers from friends and family, and also create hatred between members and nonmembers. Using slick strategies, they take money from both rich and poor individuals, especially preying on the uneducated and emotionally fragile.

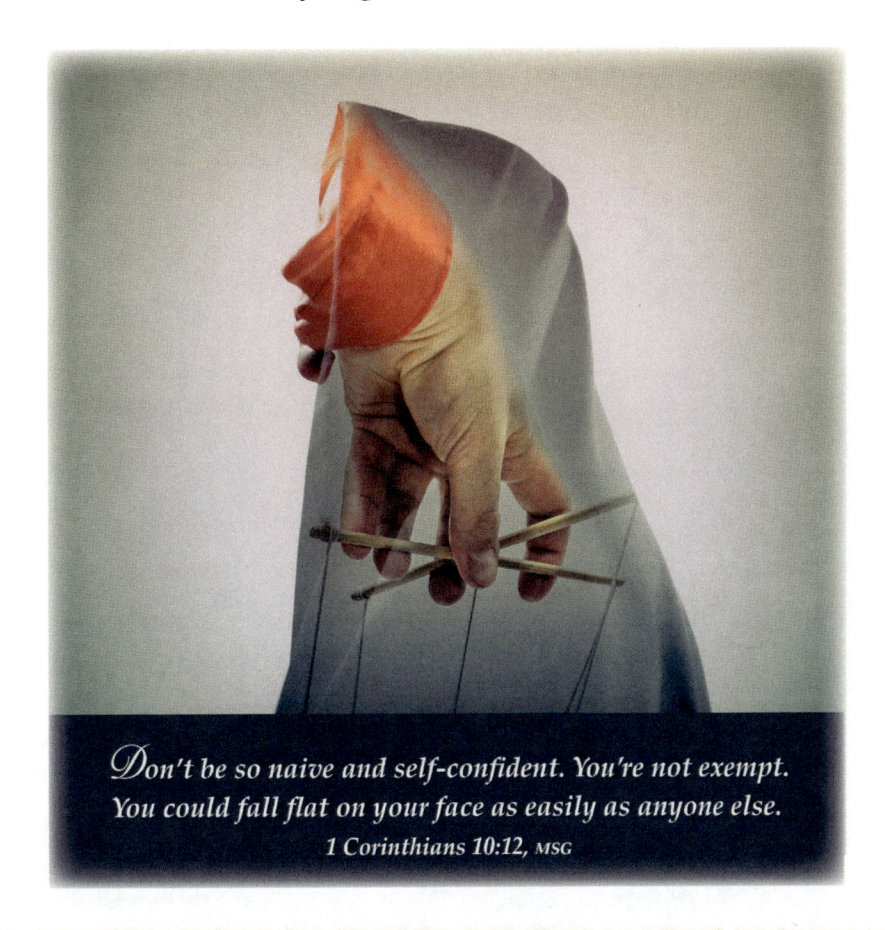

Don't be so naive and self-confident. You're not exempt. You could fall flat on your face as easily as anyone else.
1 Corinthians 10:12, MSG

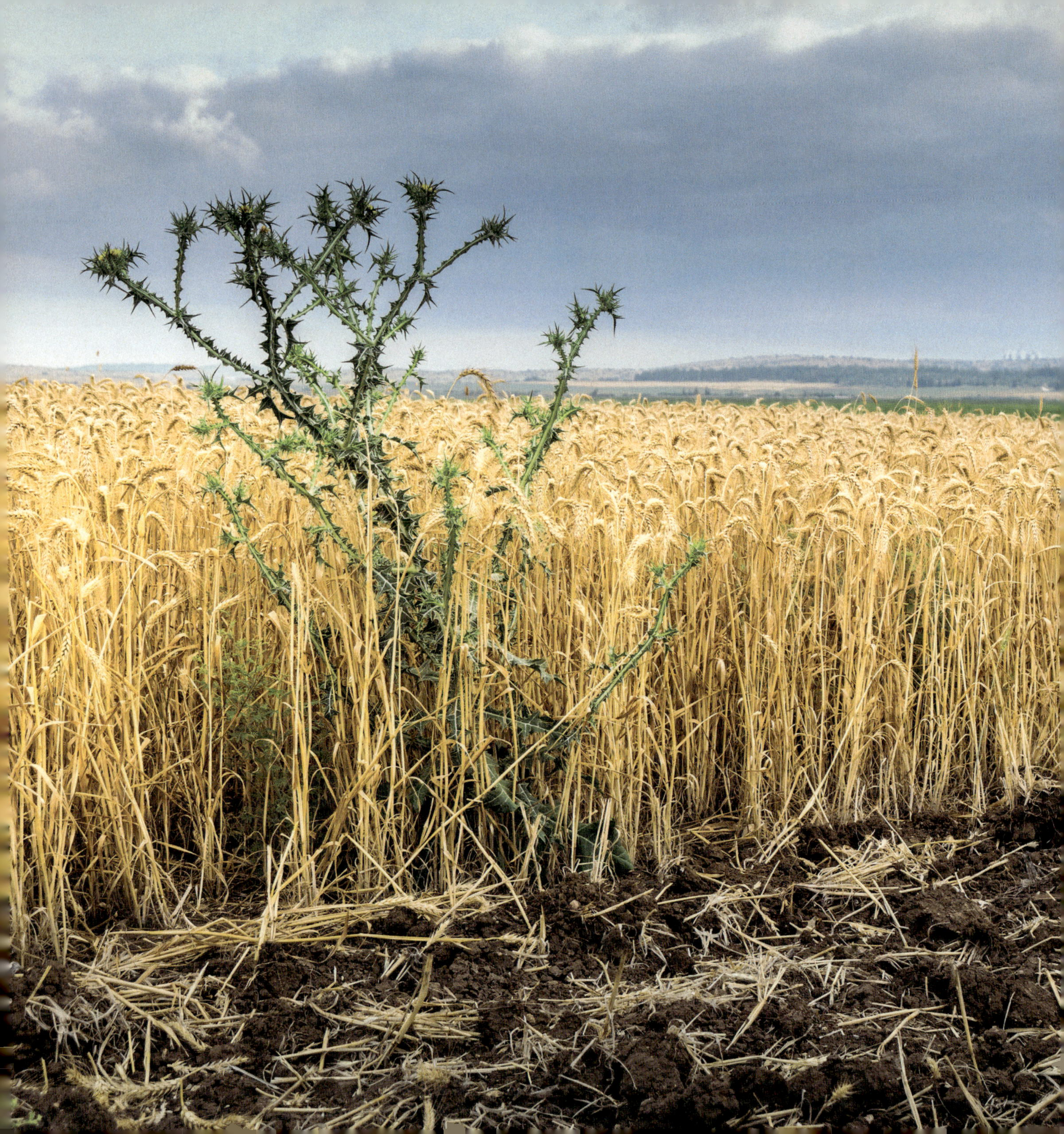

~ LETTER 16 ~

Gardener Pulls Up the Prideful Root of Falsehood

Dear Friend,

As Victoria Grace journeyed through the fiery furnace, she made another transparent confession. She admitted to wrongfully using false sources of direction during her encounter with Damien, the false teacher.

She realized that she initially made an impulsive decision to become involved with his so-called ministry. She based it on hearing the following radio announcement: *I would rather do something great for God and fail, than to do nothing and succeed.*

Read the above quote again. What jumps out at you? *Doing something great for God!*

From what we know of Victoria's character and devotion to Lord God, this statement appears to be centered on his kingdom. However, remember, Satan is always lying in wait to burrow his way into our hearts and to corrupt anything of pure and righteous intent.

How? By mingling it with self-centered pride. If not brought under submission to the Lord, this attribute leads down the path to detours, dead-ends and destruction.

Beyond the sweet fellowship that Victoria experienced with the Lord and obeying him day by day, deep in the far-reaching corners of her soul, she wanted to do something great for God and his kingdom. She rationalized her success would surely bring him maximum glory, through the outstanding accomplishments of a woman with a disability.

Early in their relationship, Damien spotted this within Victoria and cunningly encouraged her to feed upon the pride-tainted desire.

Satan's snare snapped!

Victoria recognized that Damien also succumbed to Satan's deceptive and prideful trap. His lifestyle reflected the arrogant belief that he was a "little god," supposedly possessing the big God's full power and authority.

Dear friend, whenever the devil detects even a hint of pride in people, he pounces and opens the pit for us to fall into the fiery furnace of falsehood.

This tragic deception originated in the Garden of Eden, when Satan manipulated Eve to believe that equality with God is the supreme attainment. Once Eve and Adam succumbed to this arrogant delusion, the evil one gained a foothold in the world. He continues to relentlessly deceive the human race with the same pride-driven mentality.

God "invites" us to do the extraordinary

THE SECOND MAJOR COMPONENT of Damien's skewed teaching emphasized that the goal of faith was to accomplish great things for God's kingdom. Just like everything else, he allowed Satan to twist God's Word for self-centered and prideful reasons.

As the Holy Spirit continued removing the thick fog of deception—more like smoke within a fiery furnace—from Victoria's mind, he again reminded her of God's truth. The Lord delights in *inviting* ordinary individuals to allow him to do extraordinary things, through us, for his kingdom purposes on earth.

> *For we are God's masterpiece.*
> *He has created us anew in Christ Jesus,*
> *so we can do the good things he planned for us long ago.*
> Ephesians 2:10, NLT

First, let us look at two biblical examples of godly men who sought, on their own initiative, to do something great for God—even though they had honorable motives.

Chapter seven of 2 Samuel records King David's heartfelt desire to build a majestic temple for LORD God Almighty. For hundreds of years, God chose to meet with the Israelite people inside a portable tent. Out of his great love and respect for God, King David planned to build a permanent temple in Jerusalem. He wanted God to be worshiped inside a magnificent building, worthy of his majesty and sovereignty.

However, that was not the task God called David to accomplish. Therefore, he sent the prophet Nathan to stop David's well-meaning plans. Nathan shared God's plan with David that his son Solomon would be the one to oversee the construction of the first temple (1 Kings 5:1-5).

We find a similar noble, kingdom-centered venture attempted in the New Testament. The apostle Paul, along with his evangelistic team, were commissioned by God to travel throughout the Roman empire proclaiming the gospel of Jesus Christ.

During one of their missionary journeys, described in Acts 16:6-10, they faithfully attempted to spread God's good news of forgiveness and salvation by entering two different areas. Both times they were prohibited by God's Spirit. Once getting their attention, the Holy Spirit redirected them in line with his plans and sent them into new, fertile spiritual soil.

Let us continue exploring this spiritual reality within the pages of God's Word. Whenever great events happened, did they originate within the minds and wills of people?

While in the Garden of Eden, did Adam decide on his own to pass the time by naming all of the living creatures? Did Noah come up with a wild plan to build a 450-foot ark and rescue a pair of every animal?

In a moment of feeling invincible, did Moses decide to march into the Egyptian king's palace and single-handedly release millions of Hebrew slaves? Did Deborah, a prophetess and judge, on her own authority assume the commanding position of the Israelite army and lead them to victory?

Did David, a young shepherd boy, think about becoming a powerful king and instrument in God's plan of worldwide redemption when he confronted and killed a giant with a slingshot?

Did the virgin Mary submit her résumé as a candidate to become the mother of God's Son? Did the Samaritan woman know that her kind gesture of giving Jesus a drink of water would lead to the salvation of many people?

And what about Paul—did he pull himself up by the bootstraps after being struck blind for three days and decide to become one of the most powerful Christian evangelists in history?

In all these scenarios and many more recorded in the Bible, the answer is clearly and consistently "No." It has never been God's way for individuals to seek great accomplishments on their own—even when their motives are pure in desiring to advance his kingdom.

Perhaps the most compelling example is Jesus Christ, God's own Son.

Jesus said:

"When you have lifted up the Son of Man, then you will know that I am he and that I do nothing on my own but speak just what the Father has taught me. The one who sent me is with me; he has not left me alone, for I always do what pleases him."
~ John 8:28-29, NIV

"Don't you believe that I am in the Father, and that the Father is in me? The words I say to you I do not speak on my own authority. Rather, it is the Father, living in me, who is doing his work." ~ John 14:10, NIV

If this approach in doing God's will was consistently embraced and followed by his perfect and sinless Son, then surely it is the supreme way for human beings to adopt and implement within our own daily lives.

LORD God is the initiator.
People respond to his invitation.

Jesus said, "You did not choose me, but I chose you and appointed you so that you might go and bear fruit—fruit that will last…" (John 15:16, NIV). The apostle John then wrote this in his epistle, "We love because he first loved us" (1 John 4:19, NIV).

Some people may think this approach sounds passive—that we just wait around, glancing up into the sky, until God writes our assignment in the clouds. Nothing is further from the truth.

Being responders means that we engage in daily communication with our Commander in chief, so that we are ready to adjust our lives to his direction at a moment's notice in order to accomplish his purposes. It is incredibly humbling and exciting to discover that the God who created the universe chooses us—ordinary people—to do extraordinary tasks.

Regrettably, far too many people are comfortable and satisfied with living mediocre Christian lives. We shrink back from developing a meaningful, engaging relationship with Lord God and forfeit experiencing the abundant life that he desires to give each of us.

It is important to repeat: Our active role is to cultivate a daily personal and loving relationship with our creator and Savior. We must draw close to God and let him empower us beyond our natural abilities, personalities, goals and visions. Only then are we prepared to be used as his instruments whenever he invites us to join him in his specific work, at any given time. Whatever God calls us to do, he gives us all the resources to accomplish every task.

The result is that Lord God accomplishes his extraordinary purposes in ways that only he can. Thereby, he is the one who receives maximum glory, honor and praise!

Think about it this way:

> In God's magnificent love and power, he created human beings with intelligence and creative abilities. He designed our unique personalities, talents and desires.
>
> Once individuals come into a personal relationship with Lord God, he then empowers our natural lives through his Holy Spirit to bring him glory, fulfill his promises in our lives and accomplish extraordinary kingdom-centered purposes.

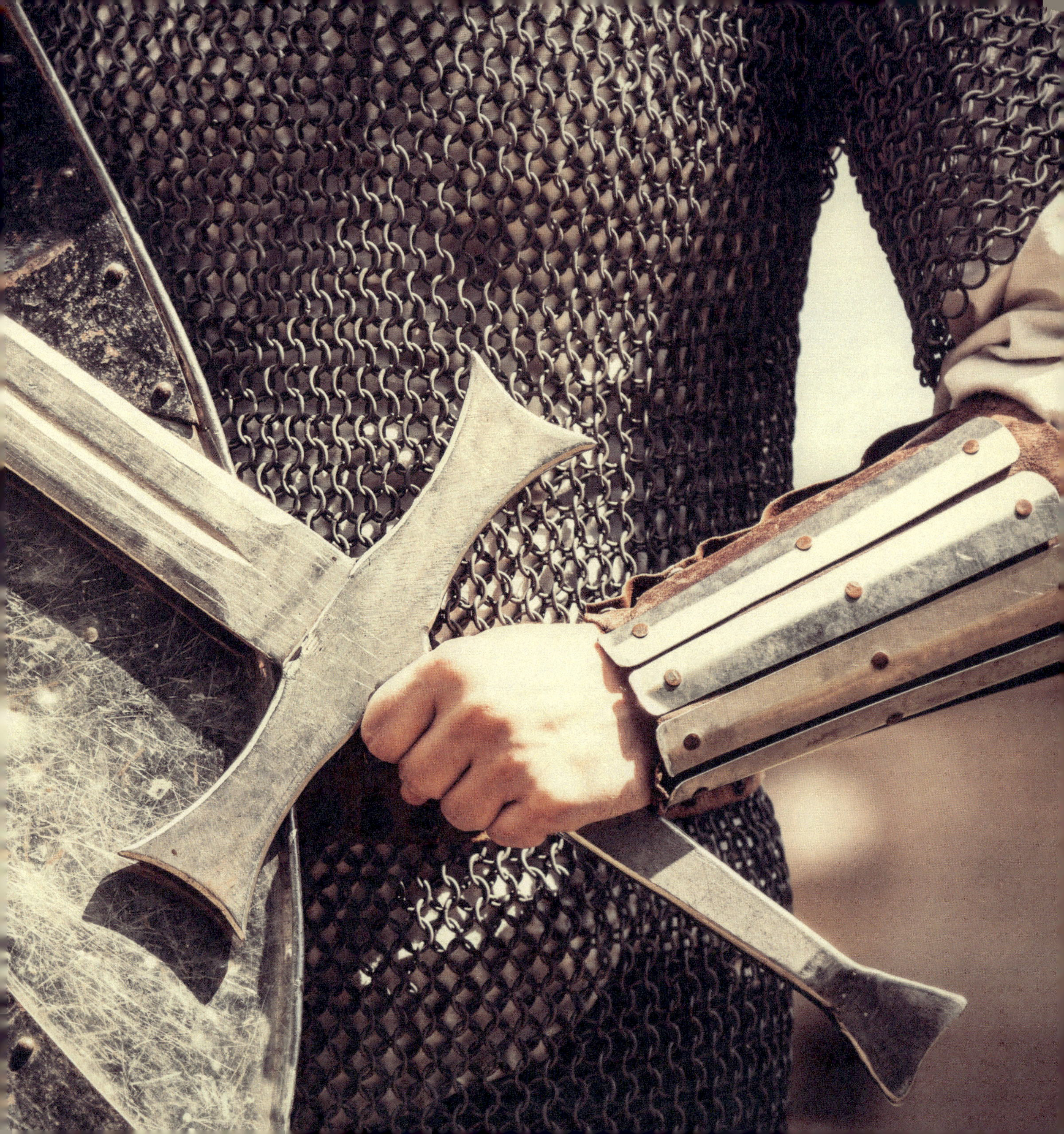

~ LETTER 17 ~
COMMANDER IN CHIEF GIVES A WAR STRATEGY TO DEFEAT SATAN AND FALSEHOOD

*D*ear Friend,

During Victoria Grace's year-long research on falsehood, she listened to valuable sermon series and read books. *[They are listed on page 132]* In this letter, she allowed me to summarize what she learned about the spiritual armor that LORD God gives us to defeat Satan and falsehood.

~ ❖ ~

IMAGINE A COUNTRY GOING TO WAR against another formidable nation.

The commander in chief calls up thousands of men and women to active duty. Once arriving at the military base, senior officers give recruits a short briefing on the attacking forces. Then, they transport the soldiers into enemy territory.

Recruits are wearing civilian clothes, because no one showed them where to get fitted for military uniforms. They were not even told that combat gear is available.

The bewildered soldiers go into battle with no uniforms, no helmets, no boots and no bulletproof vests. They have no belts to hold ammunition, knives or grenades. In fact, they are not given any weapons. They have no way of shielding themselves or fighting the enemy in close combat.

If you think this is an absurd scenario, you are absolutely right.

It would be utterly tragic to send military troops into war without first providing them thorough training and adequate equipment. This situation would never happen in military battles. If it did, the country should be found guilty of massacring its own citizens.

Regrettably, this situation is happening to members of Christ's church. When it comes to sending Christians into spiritual war against Satan and his host of evil forces, a great number of believers are tragically slain instantly, because they are not trained and equipped for battle.

On the spiritual level, our noses do not detect hints of smoke in the air. Our ears do not hear bombs exploding. Our eyes cannot see missiles aimed straight at us. Our bodies do not feel the enemy's excruciating dagger. Yet the carnage of Satan's destructive presence is everywhere.

The reality is that every person is born into the enemy's territory, because "the world around us is under Satan's power and control" (1 John 5:19, TLB). Satan is the instigator in the fierce battle for people's souls.

Once we place our trust in Jesus Christ as Savior, we are instantly transferred from the kingdom of darkness into the kingdom of light (Colossians 1:13-14). God becomes our commander in chief.

Some Christians mistakenly believe we are then removed from the war zone. This will not happen until we die and enter heaven or when Jesus returns to reign and throw Satan into tormenting hell for eternity—whichever comes first.

God gives us everything we need for victory

GOD, THE FATHER, HAS SOVEREIGN POWER to rescue his children from intense fiery furnaces of life. God, the Son, left his majestic heavenly throne to live on earth 33 years and he experienced hardships, suffering, pain and trials far beyond our ability to ever comprehend.

As a result of Christ's resurrected victory over Satan and death, he now shields his believers from being destroyed by the devil's fiery arrows. Not only that, but Christ gives everyone who places faith in him a fire-fighter's dream to eliminate the deadly smoke.

Jesus gives us a source of living water that will never fail and never be exhausted. This incredible source is God, the Holy Spirit, dwelling inside every single believer.

The Holy Spirit is to Christians like infrared scopes are to military soldiers. God's Spirit enables his combat soldiers to spot our dark and devious camouflaged enemy at any time, night or day.

Beyond giving us the constant companionship of the Holy Spirit, God also provides protective gear and weapons to engage our cunning enemy.

Ephesians 6:10-18 provides a blueprint for learning about these divine weapons. In this one passage, Lord God gives a vivid description of how to get dressed as soldiers for the unseen spiritual war raging through the centuries. *[See graphic on page 109]*

During Victoria's journey of unraveling falsehood from truth, she was drawn to one piece of the spiritual armor. It is the sword of the Spirit—Word of God.

Fellow soldier, learn to effectively use the WAR Strategy. WAR stands for Word Activated Response. As you speak to invisible, yet perilous foes, it is helpful to personalize in first person your chosen passages from God's Word.

Speak with as much force as the oncoming flaming arrows from the enemy. If for some reason you are unable to verbally speak the verses, speak them in your mind. Remember: your mind is the battleground with Satan.

Below are several spiritual weapons believers in Christ can use against Satan and his host of demons. These examples are general in nature. Whatever specific temptation or attack you face, search God's Word to find appropriate verses to deflect Satan's onslaught.

#1 Word Activated Response >> God, your every word is flawless. You are a shield to me because I take refuge in you *(based on Proverbs 30:5)*.

#2 Word Activated Response >> I am a dear child of God. I overcome falsehood because the Spirit of Jesus Christ lives inside me, and he is greater than you Satan who is in the world *(based on 1 John 4:4)*.

#3 Word Activated Response >> Lord, you are faithful. You will strengthen and protect me from the evil one *(based on 2 Thessalonians 3:3)*.

#4 Word Activated Response >> Satan, I will overcome you by the blood of the Lamb Jesus and by the word of my testimony *(based on Revelation 12:11)*.

#5 Word Activated Response >> God, keep falsehood and lies far from me *(based on Proverbs 30:8)*.

#6 Word Activated Response >> I submit myself to God. I resist you devil, and you will flee from me *(based on James 4:7)*.

#7 Word Activated Response >> Lord God, thank you for commanding your angels to guard me in all my ways *(based on Psalm 91:11)*.

#8 Word Activated Response >> Get away from me, Satan! You are a dangerous trap to me. You are seeing things merely from a human point of view, and not from God's *(based on Matthew 16:23)*.

Within the pages of the Bible, believers in Christ Jesus have an arsenal of eternal bullets to fire back at Satan during his specific and calculated attacks. We possess weapons of victory!

We must never forget that our power to conquer the evil one does not come from ourselves, nor from merely speaking words in the Bible. This is not a mechanical procedure or ritual. Our victory results directly from our personal and growing relationship with Jesus. *[See John 5:39-40]*

Once we are encapsulated by Christ's precious blood, through faith in his death and resurrection to save us, our evil adversary and his demonic forces can never destroy our souls. We are forever protected by the one true God!

In addition to using the WAR Strategy, Victoria Grace shared the following step-by-step guide. These Bible passages will help us to avoid falsehood and/or respond to it.

- Exodus 20:1-7
- 1 Timothy 4:7-8
- John 17:15-17
- 1 Corinthians 16:13
- Acts 17:11
- 1 John 4:1-6
- 1 Timothy 4:16
- James 5:19-20
- Jude 1:22-23
- Ephesians 5:6-13
- Deuteronomy 18:9-13
- Titus 3:9-11
- Proverbs 30:7-8
- Acts 20:28-31
- 1 Thessalonians 5:19-22
- Revelation 2:2-3
- Ephesians 6:10-18
- 2 John 1:9-11
- 1 Corinthians 5:9-13
- Revelation 22:18-19

Ephesians 6:10-18

Belt	➤	Truth
Breastplate	➤	Righteousness
Shoes	➤	Gospel of peace
Shield	➤	Faith
Helmet	➤	Salvation
Sword	➤	Word of God
Prayer	➤	Led by the Spirit

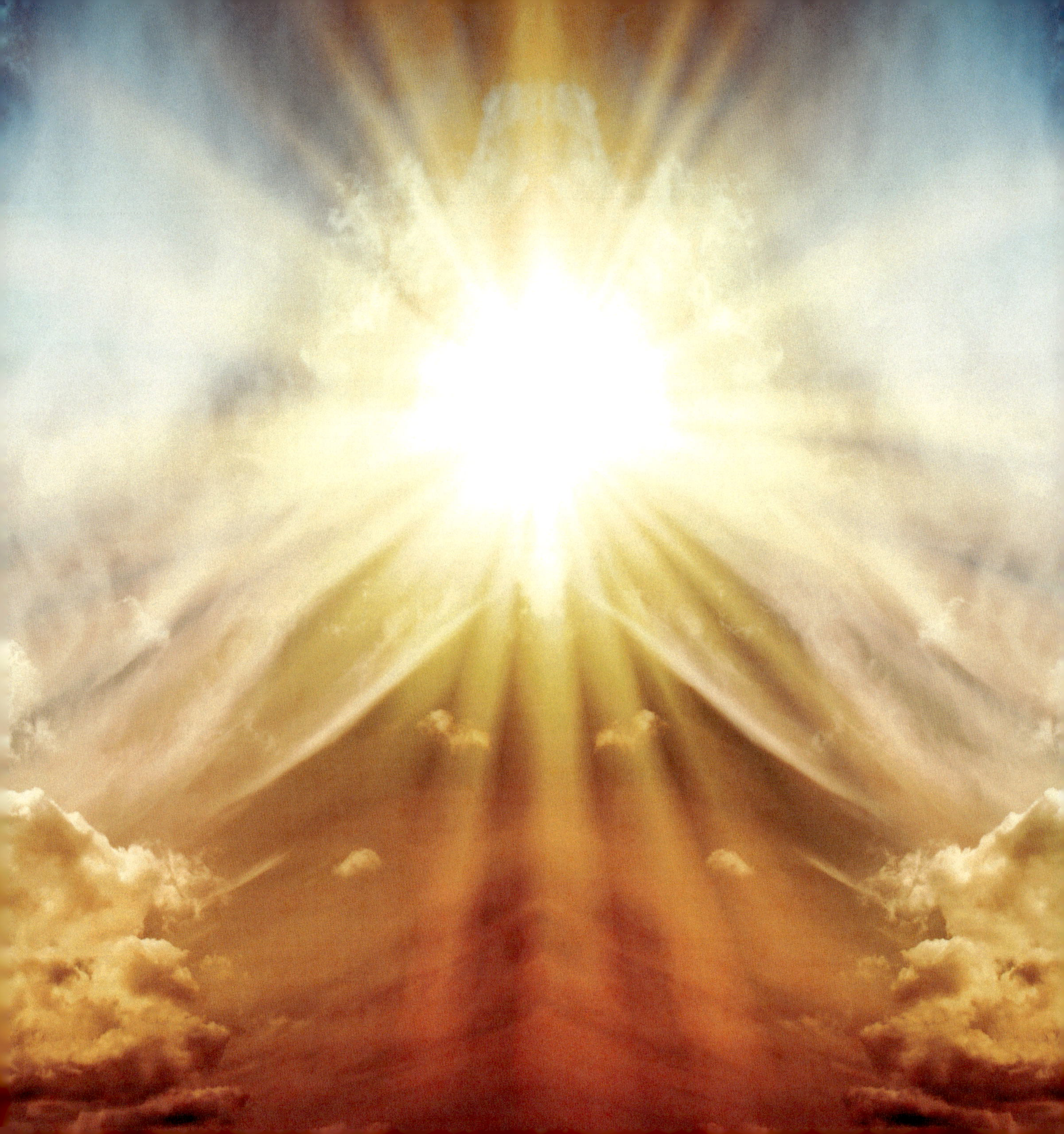

~ LETTER 18 ~

SOVEREIGN GOD RESPONDS TO PEOPLE CHOOSING TO LIVE IN FALSEHOOD

*D*ear Friend,

The apostle Paul instructs, "Do your best to present yourself to God as one approved, a worker who does not need to be ashamed and who correctly handles the word of truth" (2 Timothy 2:15, NIV).

Why? Lord God considers teaching and living truth to be an extremely serious matter. He wants to deter people around the world, throughout all generations, from engaging in falsehood and prideful living.

The Bible reveals God's response to people who mishandle his Word, and in the process victimize individuals and lead them away from the truth.

Vivid descriptions of what happens to such people include: their paths are slippery; they eat bitter food and drink poisoned water; they are scattered in different directions; they live in wastelands; they become fools; and they suffer everlasting disgrace and shame.

The Bible says that God allows all kinds of disasters and sorrows to overtake such people, with ever increasing intensity and frequency. Trouble and distress surround them. Calamity comes upon them when they least expect it.

Lord God foils the signs of false prophets and makes fools of diviners. He brings darkness over them, so that they no longer see false visions. God cuts them off from his people and he frees the victims whom false teachers ensnare.

People who consistently choose to live in pride, falsehood and defiance against God will receive what their actions deserve. His severe discipline will be upon them. Though it does not appear loving, this is indeed God's grace-filled way of bringing people back into a right relationship with himself.

God is very willing to forgive the wayward sins of all people—no matter how horrendous the iniquities. He is full of love and compassion. He is slow to anger and pronounce judgment. His tender mercies are new every morning.

At the same time, God is holy and just; he cannot fellowship with evil and sin. Thus, if people do not repent of their self-centered rebellion and sin before they die, he has no other option than to separate totally from them.

Creator God, who intimately forms each person inside the womb, hides his face from people engaged in falsehood. He withdraws his compassionate care, provision and protection. He will no longer even mention their names from his lips. All that will be left is the fearful expectation of judgment, being thrown into the eternal fiery lake of burning sulfur that is reserved for Satan, demons and the enemies of God.

In others words, God curses everyone who continues to live in falsehood. Both the person who teaches false doctrine and the one who follows the false teaching will be judged guilty.

From the beginning to the end of the Bible, Lord God remains consistent and crystal clear. "Obey all the commandments I give you. Do not add to or subtract from them" (Deuteronomy 12:32, TLB).

The apostle John warned:

> And I solemnly declare to everyone who hears the words of prophecy written in this book: If anyone adds anything to what is written here, God will add to that person the plagues described in this book. And if anyone removes any of the words from this book of prophecy, God will remove that person's share in the tree of life and in the holy city that are described in this book. ~ Revelation 22:18-19, NLT

When it comes to God's response to engaging in falsehood and victimizing people, he shows no mercy to unrepentant individuals. In the Old Testament, his harshest punishment was nothing short of execution (Deuteronomy 13:5). Equally horrifying with eternal consequences, the New Testament summarizes their destiny in Jude 1:13, "They are wild waves of the sea, foaming up their shame; wandering stars, for whom blackest darkness has been reserved forever."

With every day that passes, we are closer to the specific moment in which God will tell Jesus Christ it is time to return to earth and finally put a stop to all evil, impurity and falsehood. Some people mistakenly believe that Lord God will punish only people who unashamedly commit atrocities against their fellow human beings or scandalously pervert God's Word.

"The wrath of God is being revealed from heaven against all the godlessness and wickedness of people, who suppress the truth by their wickedness" (Romans 1:18, NIV).

> *The* coming of the lawless one will be in accordance with how Satan works. He will use all sorts of displays of power through signs and wonders that serve the lie, and all the ways that wickedness deceives those who are perishing. They perish because they refused to love the truth and so be saved. For this reason God sends them a powerful delusion so that they will believe the lie and so that all will be condemned who have not believed the truth but have delighted in wickedness.
>
> ~ 2 Thessalonians 2:9-12, NIV

Read the two Bible passages again. Lord God's wrath will be executed because of three reasons: ◆ **People suppress the truth.** ◆ **People refuse to love the truth.** ◆ **People do not believe the truth.**

"Don't be misled—you cannot mock the justice of God. You will always harvest what you plant" (Galatians 6:7, NLT). If people sow seeds of falsehood into their lives and other people's lives, then they will reap a harvest of falsehood. The cost will be utter destruction and eternal torment.

Although such consequences are tragic, they are the direct result of people hardening their hearts toward God and remaining deceived in their minds. It is not what God desires. Can you hear his heart in the following verse?

> *As* sure as I am the living God,
> I take no pleasure from the death of the wicked.
> I want the wicked to change their ways and live.
> Turn your life around! Reverse your evil ways!
> Ezekiel 33:11, MSG

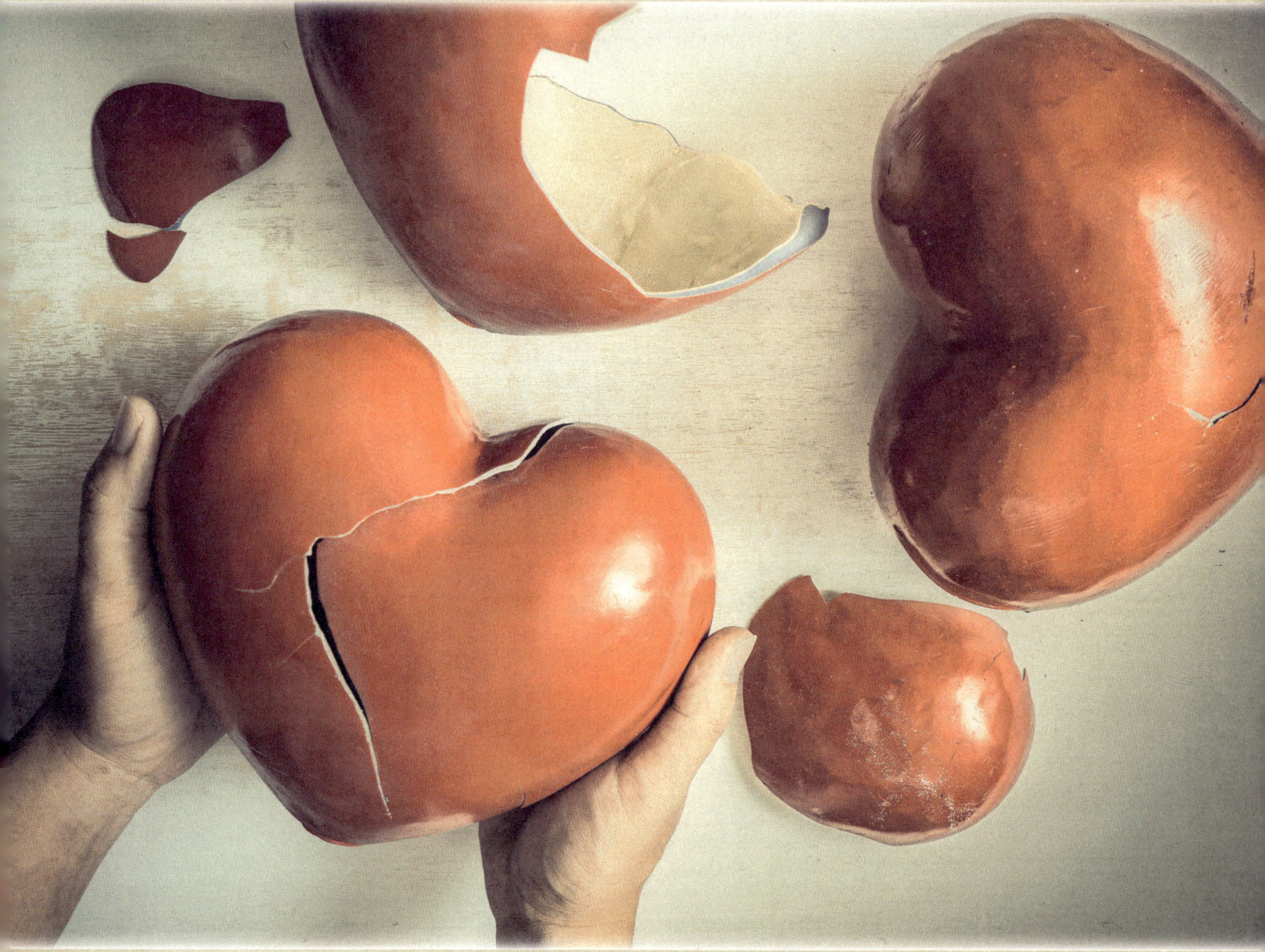

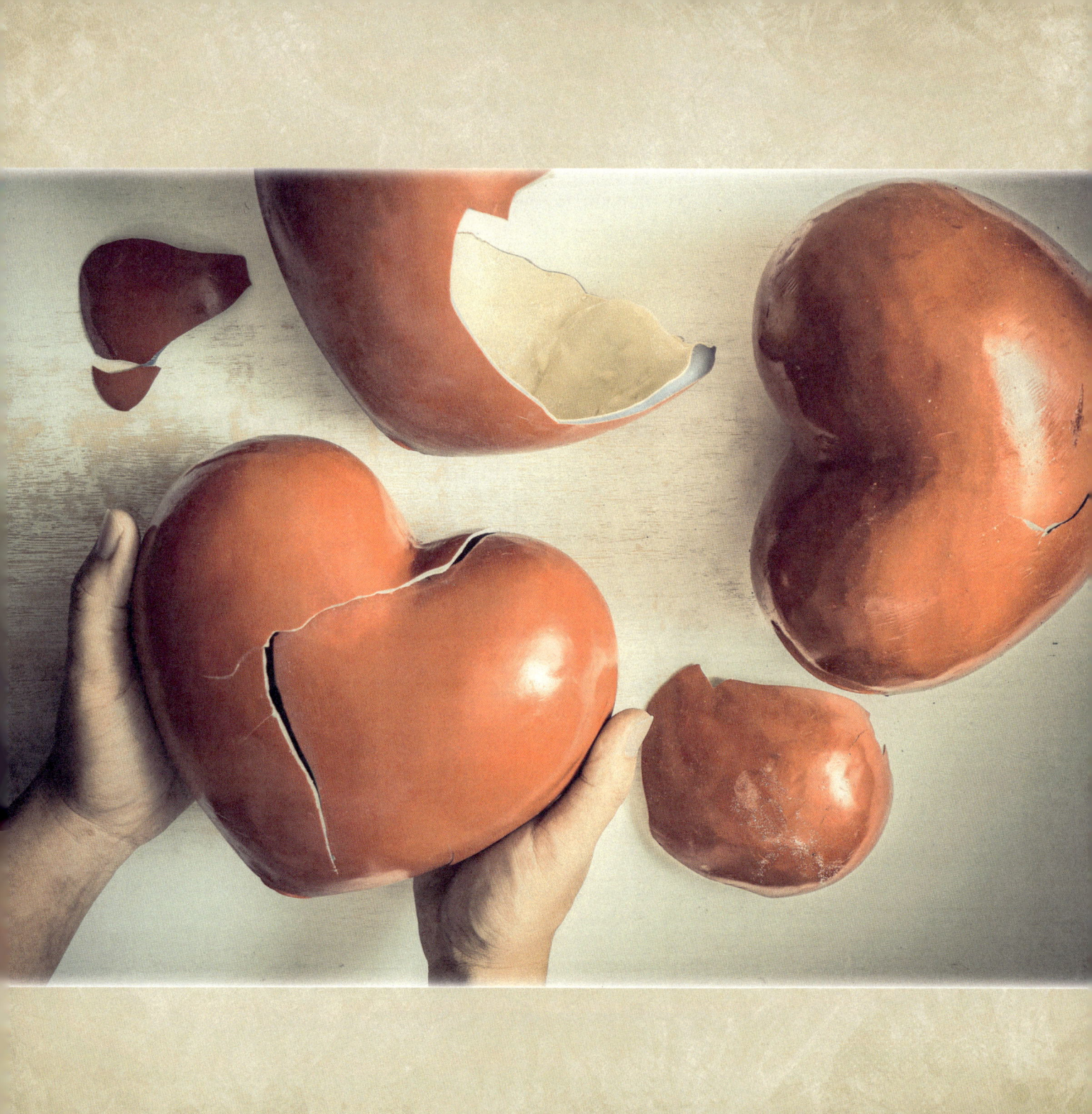

~ LETTER 19 ~

GREAT PHYSICIAN LEADS US THROUGH THE HEALING OF OUR SOULS

*D*ear Friend,

The human soul does not heal thoroughly unless we walk through specific stages of healing, which are ultimately designed by God. Bypassing or accelerating necessary stages results in harmful effects.

Failure to grieve completely leads to emotional problems later. Many times, our bodies reveal external evidence through health problems. Relationships are damaged through anger, bitterness, revenge and other emotions mixed together into an internal poison.

Have you ever thought about how a wound goes through many healing stages?

In this epistle, Victoria Grace has transparently shared many stages that she journeyed with Lord God healing her wounded soul, after her fiery furnace experience with the false teacher. The Holy Spirit gave her an analogy to help understand the healing process.

Let us ponder this intriguing analogy, because it can be applied during our own times of pain, suffering and brokenness.

Suppose you accidentally sliced your thumb with a knife. The knife removed some of your skin, but the cut is not deep enough to require stitches. You are extremely conscious of the wound for the first several days after the incident. It requires your daily attention to clean, medicate and bandage.

Occasionally, the memory of the unexpected accident pops into your mind. You are left dealing with the throbbing effects as you attempt to return to life as usual.

One day, to your surprise, you discover a scab completely covering the once open wound. You decide that it is time to remove the clumsy bandage. A sense of freedom lifts your restricted spirit. You just want to get back into the normal routine of living.

Oops! As you start working freely again with your hands, the edge of the crusty scab gets caught on what is usually a harmless object. In the blink of an eye, the protective covering rips off. You experience a surge of pain. Glancing at your thumb, you are shocked to see bright red blood dripping onto your clothes.

A wave of disappointment floods your body. You think the healing process must start all over. However, that is not true.

Suppose you had the ability to enter inside your thumb and look out. Your perspective of the wound would dramatically change. You could begin to understand that healing always starts inside and slowly moves outward.

The forming of a scab is the visible evidence of the invisible healing taking place on the inside. Therefore, when your scab was accidentally knocked off, much healing already had occurred internally.

Several weeks pass. Perhaps something else happens to knock off yet another scab. You become frustrated and weary in dealing with this cycle.

More time passes. A sense of victory swells through you as one day you notice layers of new skin encircling the shrinking scab. Then, you jam the injured thumb while closing your desk drawer. No blood appears, because by this time your skin has grown together. Yet a dull pain still registers in your brain.

For the next month or so, your injured thumb remains tender to the touch. To people around you, your initial injury has long since been forgotten and they are now oblivious to your sensitive area of healing.

Perhaps your knife wound will leave a scar for some time. However, little by little all of the tenderness and redness disappear. You finally regain full use of your thumb without reliving the injury. Life moves forward.

Now stop for a moment and change the above description from the healing of your thumb to the healing of your soul. Your soul consists of your mind, will and emotions. Spiritual and emotional healing are as much a process as physical healing.

> *God is the only one who knows the arrival, duration and impact of our distinct crises. In the same way Jesus Christ, the Great Physician, is the only one who knows how to completely heal our wounded souls.*

The Great Physician's specialty is mending the brokenhearted, proclaiming freedom for the captives, releasing prisoners from darkness, comforting all who mourn and providing for those who grieve (Isaiah 61:1-3).

"What a glorious Lord! He who daily bears our burdens also gives us our salvation" (Psalm 68:19, TLB).

The healing of our wounded souls is available at our asking. Start the process now by believing and praying, "Lord, you alone can heal me, you alone can save, and my praises are for you alone" (Jeremiah 17:14, TLB).

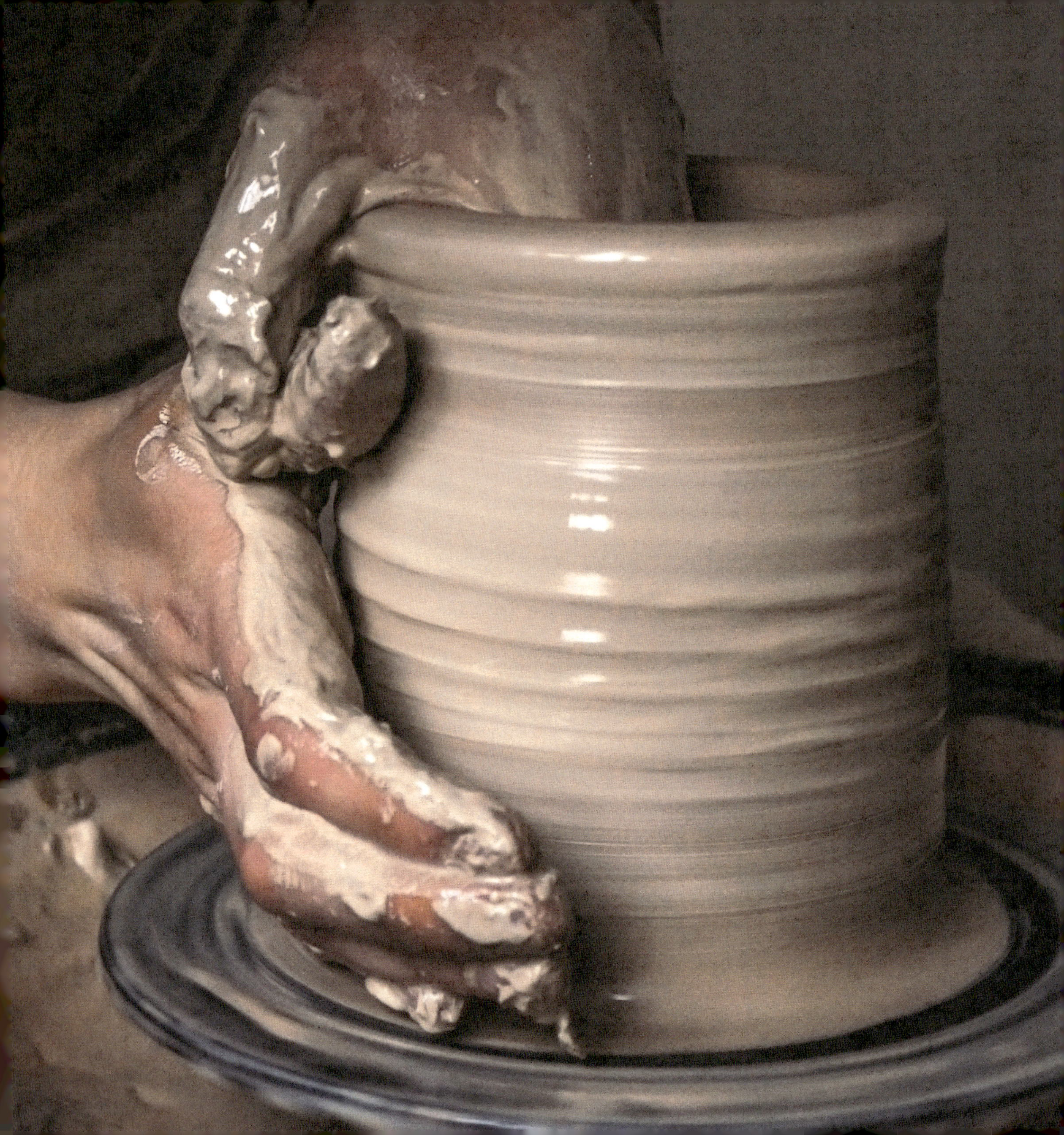

~ LETTER 20 ~

Master Potter Shares the Process of Molding His Clay

*D*ear Friend,

Within the pages of this epistle, we have discovered many names and characteristics of God. After Victoria shared her journey with me, I visited a pottery shop to acquire a better understanding of how God, the Master Potter, relates to each of us as his clay.

The following descriptive summary is the result of spending time with the shop's potter, watching and listening to him explain his skilled trade.

> *Yet you, Lord, are our Father. We are the clay, you are the potter;*
> *we are all the work of your hand.*
> Isaiah 64:8, NIV

The potter starts with a slab of hard clay. He throws it down onto a hard surface repeatedly to remove air bubbles and eliminate defects. He examines the compressed clay as he mixes in softer clay to reduce stiffness and reach a desired consistency.

The potter cuts the hunk of clay into pieces, softening one clump with the warmth of his hands. He kneads it as a baker prepares dough, squeezing and rolling it into a ball, and weighing the lump for his intended purpose.

The potter places the clay on the center of the wheel and pours water on top of the round mass as he adjusts the speed of the spinning wheel.

The potter applies pressure with his hands and fingers to the clay, reaching down into its center and expanding it from the inside. He adds water frequently to reduce friction, and cradles the clay inside both his hands, molding its shape with external and internal forces.

The potter fashions his work. He observes an emerging shape rise from the wheel. It becomes a bowl, plate, cup or pitcher. It is created to be practical or decorative. The potter knows that the final design is his, not the clay's.

The potter prepares the pottery for the kiln by cutting away excess clay that is not needed. He carves into its surface his own signature, smoothing rough edges and sponging it with more water. He lets it dry in the open air within his protective care.

The potter places his unique creation inside the kiln and sets the temperature to 2,300 degrees. He leaves it inside the blistering heat, knowing it becomes stronger and more useful the longer it remains in the fire.

The potter removes his precious pottery from the kiln after shutting it off at the designated time. He lets the piece cool for another day, reusing specks of discarded clay.

The potter celebrates his finished creation. He delights in the fact that no two pieces are exactly alike, and that the pottery will be used to serve people in ways that he planned from the very beginning.

Savior God will transform you, too!

DEAR FRIEND, LORD GOD ALMIGHTY not only saves people from our sins for all eternity, but he also rescues us. In 2 Peter 2:9, the apostle reminds us that God knows exactly how to rescue his children from trials.

Be careful not to limit God by expecting him to rescue and heal you in the same way he worked in the life of Victoria Grace. Neither anticipate that he will work in ways as he does in the lives of your family and friends. Do not even look for God to rescue you in the manner that he healed you in the past.

The Lord desires to love, care, heal and interact with each of us in deeply personal ways. Total healing requires continual surrendering to the mighty and transforming power of the Master Potter.

*Celebrate the tremendous significance
of God's ability to transform your fiery furnaces
into beacons from which his glorious light
of truth shatters Satan's darkness.*

Bible Verses to Study

Identity of One True God

Numbers ~
  23:19
Deuteronomy ~
  4:32-35
  4:39
  6:4
1 Kings ~
  8:60
1 Chronicles ~
  16:25-26
2 Chronicles ~
  15:3-4
Isaiah ~
  37:16
  42:8
  43:10-13
  44:6
  45:5-7
  45:12
  45:14
  45:18-24
  46:9-10
  48:2-3
  48:12-13
  66:1-2

Jeremiah ~
  10:6-7
  10:10-13
  32:27
  33:2
  51:15-16
  51:19
Daniel ~
  3:28-29
Hosea ~
  13:4
Joel ~
  2:27
Malachi ~
  2:10
Mark ~
  12:29-32
John ~
  5:18
  10:27-30
  12:44-45
  17:3
  18:37
Acts ~
  4:12
  4:24
  17:23-31

Romans ~
  3:29-30
  9:5
1 Corinthians ~
  8:5-6
Ephesians ~
  4:6
Colossians ~
  1:15-20
  2:9-10
1 Thessalonians ~
  1:9-10
1 Timothy ~
  1:17
  2:5-6
James ~
  2:19
1 John ~
  5:20
Revelation ~
  1:8
  21:6
  22:13

Bible Verses to Study

Satan

Genesis ~
  3:1-7
Job ~
  1:6-12
Isaiah ~
  14:12-15
Ezekiel ~
  28:11-19
Zechariah ~
  3:1
Matthew ~
  4:1-11
  12:24
  13:19
  13:38-39
  25:41
Mark ~
  3:22
Luke ~
  10:18
John ~
  8:44
  10:10
  16:11
  17:15
2 Corinthians ~
  2:11
  4:4
  6:14-15
  11:3
  11:14-15
Ephesians ~
  2:2
  4:26-27
  6:11-12
  6:16
1 Thessalonians ~
  3:5
2 Timothy ~
  2:26
Hebrews ~
  2:14
1 Peter ~
  5:8
1 John ~
  3:8
  5:18-19
Revelation ~
  9:11
  12:3
  12:7-17
  20:2-3
  20:10

Exalting Oneself to Level of God

Isaiah ~
  47:8-11
Daniel ~
  4:28-37
  11:36-45

Pride

Deuteronomy ~
  8:17-18
Psalms ~
  5:4-6
  81:9-14
Proverbs ~
  1:23-31
  3:34
  6:16-19
  8:13
  10:9
  14:12
  16:5
  16:18
  21:4
  29:1

Bible Verses to Study

Pride

Ecclesiastes ~
  8:7-8
Isaiah ~
  2:11-12
  3:16
  5:18-25
  10:12-19
  13:11
  25:11
  47:8
Jeremiah ~
  5:21-22
  9:23-24
  18:11-12
  44:16-18
  50:31-32
Ezekiel ~
  35:13-14
Daniel ~
  4:37
  5:18-31
Hosea ~
  10:13-14
  13:6
Luke ~
  14:11
James ~
  4:4-6

False Gods

Exodus ~
  20:3-6
  34:12-17
Leviticus ~
  19:4
Deuteronomy ~
  4:15-19
  12:31-32
  17:2-5
  28:64
1 Kings ~
  14:9
2 Kings ~
  17:29
  17:38-39
1 Chronicles ~
  16:25-26
Psalms ~
  4:2
  115:2-8
Isaiah ~
  41:21-24
  45:20
Jeremiah ~
  2:11
  2:28
Ezekiel ~
  8:5-16

Daniel ~
  5:4
  11:8
Hosea ~
  13:1-3
Habakkuk ~
  2:18-19
Matthew ~
  6:24
Acts ~
  7:39-43
  17:16
  17:22-23
1 Corinthians ~
  8:4-6
  10:14
  10:18-22
  12:2
2 Corinthians ~
  6:16
Colossians ~
  3:5-6
1 John ~
  5:21
Revelation ~
  2:14
  9:20

Bible Verses to Study

False Sources of Direction

Exodus ~ 28:30 Leviticus ~ 8:8 19:26 19:31 20:6 20:27 Deuteronomy ~ 18:9-14 Numbers ~ 27:21 1 Samuel ~ 14:37-44 28:3-20 30:7-8 2 Kings ~ 9:22 21:6 23:24 1 Chronicles ~ 26:13-16	2 Chronicles ~ 33:6 Nehemiah ~ 11:1 Psalms ~ 22:18 Proverbs ~ 16:33 Isaiah ~ 8:19-20 19:3-4 44:9-20 47:12-15 Jeremiah ~ 27:9 29:8-9 Ezekiel ~ 21:21 Daniel ~ 2:1-12 2:27-28 5:5-8	Hosea ~ 4:10-12 Jonah ~ 1:7 Micah ~ 3:5-7 Nahum ~ 3:4 Zechariah ~ 10:2 Matthew ~ 27:35 John ~ 19:23-24 Acts ~ 1:26 19:17-19 Galatians ~ 5:19-21 Revelation ~ 22:14-15

Casting Lots: *This practice was used by pagans. God allowed his people to also use lots, Urim and Thummim for a period of time to give them divine direction. God stopped this practice right before he gave them the Holy Spirit, providing them with constant divine direction from henceforth.*

Bible Verses to Study

False Prophets and Teachers

Deuteronomy ~
13:1-18
18:20-22
Isaiah ~
5:18-21
9:14-16
28:15
30:1
30:8-13
32:6-7
41:22-24
47:9-15
Jeremiah ~
2:26-27
5:1-3
5:23-31
6:13-15
7:4-11
8:8-12
9:8
14:14-16
23:9-40
27:14-18
29:8-9
Lamentations ~
2:14
Ezekiel ~
22:25-29

Micah ~
3:5-7
Zephaniah ~
3:4
Malachi ~
2:7-9
3:13-18
Matthew ~
7:15-23
24:3-11
24:23-25
Mark ~
12:38-40
13:5-6
13:21-23
Luke ~
6:26
Acts ~
20:28-31
Romans ~
16:17-18
1 Corinthians ~
15:33
2 Corinthians ~
2:17
10:12
11:3-4

11:12-15
11:19-20
Galatians ~
1:6-9
2:4-5
3:1
4:16-17
5:7-10
6:12
Ephesians ~
4:14
Colossians ~
2:4
2:8
2:18-23
2 Thessalonians ~
2:1-4
1 Timothy ~
1:3-7
1:18-20
4:1-7
6:3-10
6:20-21
2 Timothy ~
2:17-18
3:1-9
3:13
4:3-4
4:14-15

Bible Verses to Study

False Prophets and Teachers

Titus ~
 1:10-16
Hebrews ~
 13:9
2 Peter ~
 2:1-22
 3:3-7
 3:16-17
1 John ~
 2:4-6
 2:18-19
 2:26-27
 3:6-10
 4:1-8
2 John ~
 1:7-11
Jude ~
 1:3-19
Revelation ~
 2:20-24
 16:13-14
 19:19-20
 20:9-10

Tampering with the Bible

Deuteronomy ~
 12:32
Proverbs ~
 30:5-6
Revelation ~
 22:18-19

Combat Satan's Attacks

Matthew ~
 6:13
1 Corinthians ~
 10:12
2 Corinthians ~
 10:3-5
Ephesians ~
 6:10-18
James ~
 4:7-8
1 Peter ~
 5:6-9

Trust God to Bring Justice; Do Not Retaliate

Psalms ~
 37:7-8
Romans ~
 12:17-21
Ephesians ~
 4:26-27
1 Peter ~
 2:21-23
 3:9-11

Love, Forgive and Pray for Your Enemies

Matthew ~
 6:12
 6:14-15
Luke ~
 6:27-37
Colossians ~
 3:12-14

Bible Verses to Study

God's Response to Falsehood

Deuteronomy ~
  11:16-17
  13:1-11
  18:19-22
  30:16-18
  31:18
Joshua ~
  23:16
Judges ~
  10:13-14
Psalms ~
  16:4
Isaiah ~
  30:9-14
  42:17
  44:24-26
Jeremiah ~
  1:16
  8:8-13
  13:24-25
  17:5-6
  23:9-40
  25:4-7
  50:36
Ezekiel ~
  6:1-14
  11:21
  12:24-28
  13:1-23
  14:1-11
  20:39
  22:3-4
  30:13
Hosea ~
  2:13
  2:17
Amos ~
  2:4-5
  5:26-27
Micah ~
  3:5-12
  5:10-15
Zephaniah ~
  1:4-6
  2:10-11
Zechariah ~
  13:1-3
Malachi ~
  3:5
Matthew ~
  23:13-36
Mark ~
  9:42
  12:24
Romans ~
  1:18-32
  2:5-11
2 Thessalonians ~
  2:1-12
2 Timothy ~
  2:17-19
Titus ~
  1:11
  1:13
  3:9-11
Hebrews ~
  6:4-6
  10:26-31
Jude ~
  1:12-13
Revelation ~
  2:20-23
  19:20
  20:10
  21:7-8
  22:13-15

Bible Verses to Study

God's Higher Purposes for Painful Trials

Psalms ~
 119:71
Luke ~
 22:31-32
John ~
 9:1-3
 11:4
Romans ~
 8:17-19
2 Corinthians ~
 1:3-5
 1:8-11
 3:18
 4:7-10
 4:16-18
 12:8-10
Hebrews ~
 12:10-11
1 Peter ~
 1:6-7
 4:12-16
 5:10

Remember God's Faithfulness in the Past and His Promises

Psalms ~
 40:5
 105:5
 143:3-5
Isaiah ~
 46:9
Ephesians ~
 2:12-13

Hebrews ~
 10:32-38
Jude ~
 1:17-21

Continue Talking with God in Prayer

Psalms ~
 4:3
 66:20
Isaiah ~
 30:19
Matthew ~
 26:41
John ~
 15:4-5

Philippians ~
 4:6-7
1 Thessalonians ~
 5:16-18
2 Thessalonians ~
 3:2

Bible Verses to Study

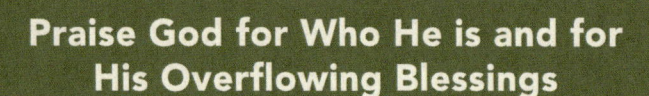

Praise God for Who He is and for His Overflowing Blessings

Nehemiah ~
  9:5-6
Psalms ~
  16:7-8
  18:46
  30:4-5
  42:11
  47:6-8
  51:15-17
  56:4
  59:16-17
  68:19-20
  71:14-16
  86:12-15
  96:4-6
  105:1-4
  139:14-18
  145:3
  147:1-11
Isaiah ~
  25:1
Jeremiah ~
  20:13
Ephesians ~
  1:3
Hebrews ~
  13:15
1 Peter ~
  1:3-5
Revelation ~
  4:11

Trust God and Do Not Fret

Psalms ~
  37:1-7
  40:4
  118:4-9
Proverbs ~
  3:5-6
  24:19-20

Move Forward in Life and Faith

Isaiah ~
  43:18-19
Philippians ~
  3:12-14

Believe God to Save and Transform Your Circumstances

Isaiah ~
  25:9
Romans ~
  8:28
  10:9-13
2 Thessalonians ~
  3:3
2 Timothy ~
  4:18
Hebrews ~
  11:6
1 Peter ~
  1:8-9
  1:13

REFERENCES

❖

Bob Russell and Rusty Russell, *Jesus: Lord of Your Personality* (West Monroe, Louisiana: Howard Pub., 2002), 70.

David Reagan, "The Deception of the Cults," *Lamplighter* (McKinney, Texas: Lamb and Lion Ministries, October 1999). https://christinprophecy.org/articles/the-deception-of-the-cults/

Stephen Arterburn and David Stoop, *Seven Keys to Spiritual Renewal* (Wheaton, Illinois: Tyndale House Publishers, 1998), 111-113.

Stephen Arterburn, "Seven Keys to Spiritual Renewal" (Santa Cruz, Calif.: Living on the Edge with Chip Ingram, 2/20/02).

Warren Wiersbe, source unknown.

Resources

❖

Anne Graham Lotz, *The Vision of His Glory*

Beth Moore, *When Godly People Do Ungodly Things*—workbook

Bob George, *Classic Christianity*

Charles F. Stanley, "False Teachers" (In Touch Ministries, cassette AV187)

Charles F. Stanley, "New Age Movement" and "Occult," *The Glorious Journey*

Chip Ingram, *The Invisible War*

Dan Vander Lugt, *What in the World is Satan Doing?*

David Jeremiah, *A Bend in the Road*

Dee Brestin and Kathy Troccoli, *Falling in Love with Jesus*—workbook

Frank Minirth, Paul Meier and Stephen Arterburn, *The Complete Life Encyclopedia*

Henry T. Blackaby and Claude V. King, *Experiencing God*—workbook

Josh McDowell and Don Stewart, *Handbook of Today's Religions*

Karl Alsin, "When Cults Come Knocking," *Discipleship Journal*

Rick Warren, *The Purpose-Driven Life*

Ron Carlson and Ed Decker, *Fast Facts on False Teachings*

Walter Martin, *The Kingdom of the Cults*

Ward Patterson, "A Celebration of Forgiveness," *The Lookout*

Wendy Lawton, "Lessons from Clay," *Discipleship Journal*

Author & Designer of the Book

Jennifer Lynn Heck has taken various leaps of faith throughout her life. It includes seven tandem skydives, one at 15,000 feet.

She is the author and designer of two books. *A Heavenly Conversation One Night Before Christmas* was a #1 bestseller on Amazon in 2021 and 2022. Her second book is *Walking Victoriously Through a Fiery Furnace,* published in 2023.

For nearly thirty years, Jennifer worked as a graphic designer and has written more than 130 articles for Christian publications.

Jennifer graduated from the University of Louisville with a bachelor's degree in Business Administration; Louisville, Kentucky. She earned a second bachelor's degree from Johnson Bible College; Knoxville, Tennessee. Her major was the Bible and she specialized in disability ministry.

Book Endorsements & Reviews

❖

*A*uthor Jennifer Lynn Heck has written a powerful story from a real-life experience. In her book, *Walking Victoriously Through a Fiery Furnace,* she brings the characters to life on each page. You won't want to put this book down, until you read how the story unfolds.

Jennifer concludes the book with lessons Victoria Grace learned, as she walked through a fiery furnace of betrayal and false teaching. She also shares how you can practically overcome any painful trial—through a relationship with Jesus Christ. As you follow along this journey, you will discover how to heal from suffering and broken relationships in your own life.

DAVE STONE, Retired Senior Pastor
Southeast Christian Church; Louisville, Kentucky

*I*n this epistle, Jennifer Lynn Heck shares how challenging it can be to navigate between truth and falsehood. *Walking Victoriously Through a Fiery Furnace* tells the true story of Victoria Grace. She is a victim—but more significantly, she is a victor. We quickly discover that Victoria could be any one of us.

In today's culture, this story is so very relevant. I certainly need the constant reminder and encouragement that truth is not subjective. God is Truth! This book is a road map to fully entrusting your heart and care to Him.

TONI ROSE, Co-founder & Executive Director of
GrowingYourMarriage.org; Louisville, Kentucky

*I*n 1978, the world was shocked when 909 members of a cult committed mass suicide. In the years since, we have witnessed other tragedies caused by cultic leaders. We ask, "How can people be so deeply deceived?"

In this book—based on true life experience—Jennifer Lynn Heck gives amazing insight into the seductive and destructive power of false teaching. She doesn't stop there. Through her gripping and creative narrative, Jennifer offers guidance and hope for the God-empowered journey towards healing and a restoration of joy.

Continued >>

Book Endorsements & Reviews

❖

I highly recommend all Christians read *Walking Victoriously Through a Fiery Furnace*. This short, fast-paced book is packed with applications to our lives and biblical encouragement, instruction and warnings. The topical lists of Scripture verses, in the appendix, provide an excellent resource for personal or group study.

DAVID WHEELER, Seminar Presenter at LegacyCoalition.com, Retired Pastor and University Professor; Knoxville, Tennessee

The book, *Walking Victoriously Through a Fiery Furnace*, delves deep into the trenches of the sometimes messy parts of the Christian walk. Just as God used the heart wrenching experiences of Jeremiah and Job to impart wisdom to believers throughout the ages, God is using Victoria Grace's experience to teach followers of Jesus difficult lessons in spiritual warfare, healing from spiritual trauma, and forgiveness.

Author Jennifer Lynn Heck uses the literary style of an epistle to connect Victoria's tough walk and subsequent victory in a way that readers can apply to their own circumstances.

SHEILA SANDERS, Registered Nurse; Louisville, Kentucky

God's Word is clear: suffering is part of the Christian faith. The majority of people avoid any type of suffering at all costs. Some people have learned to embrace suffering as an opportunity to grow in their relationship with the Lord and serve people.

Jennifer Lynn Heck is one of those individuals. Her book, *Walking Victoriously Through a Fiery Furnace*, tells the triumphant story of Victoria Grace. The Bible verse Genesis 50:20 says it best, "You intended to harm me, but God intended it for good to accomplish what is now being done…"

Readers of Jennifer's book will become equipped to avoid false teachers and live God's truth. She also guides and encourages readers through the healing process in their own suffering and fiery furnace trials.

CHAD RUSSELL, Realtor/Licensed Broker at Re/Max, Co-host of Solid Steps Radio; Louisville, Kentucky

Book Endorsements & Reviews

❖

Walking Victoriously Through a Fiery Furnace is a raw, true story of Victoria Grace—a dedicated believer in Jesus Christ, who finds herself caught in the trap of a false teacher. She is not alone. False teachers thrive around the world. They are dangerous!

Author Jennifer Lynn Heck tells this hard story to warn others, helping them identify and shun those individuals who mix lies with biblical truth. Her powerful book is also a guide for everyone wondering how to heal from deep wounds of betrayal.

Speaking from firsthand knowledge, more than 50 years ago, I was caught up in the drama of a false teacher. Ironically, he was the one who led me to Jesus. I walked away from my secure job to follow him. I wrote his books, brochures and teachings—for pennies. Thousands of other people followed him, too. It took years for me to realize that this man's teaching was laced with lies. It took additional years for me to recover.

My prayer is that Jennifer's bold, yet compassionate, book will help individuals heal from their wounds. Oh, how it must grieve God when people, who pretend to follow Him, twist the truth and victimize other people!

RUTH SCHENK, Professional Writer; Louisville, Kentucky

Jennifer Lynn Heck is a talented and gifted writer. Her words build pictures in my mind. This book tells the captivating story of Victoria Grace. I had to force myself to set it aside, rather than read it all in one day. It was partly because I relate to being betrayed and having a close encounter with a false teacher/prophet.

In this multifaceted book, Jennifer vividly shares Victoria's hurt, disappointment and pain and also challenges readers to consider our source of value and worth. Jennifer sets a firm foundation for trusting Father God, in spite of our desires and circumstances.

We are all vulnerable and need to be on guard, taking every thought captive and holding it up to the light of God's Word. Scripture warns us that Satan and his servants masquerade as angels of light—not in the world (they don't need to be in disguise in the world), but inside the church! They look and sound righteous, but they are not.

Walking Victoriously Through a Fiery Furnace is a timely book written to an unprepared, immature body of Christ—the church.

LINDA CHILDRESS, Certified Life Coach; New Albany, Indiana

Book Endorsements & Reviews

❖

In the book, *Walking Victoriously Through a Fiery Furnace,* author Jennifer Lynn Heck creatively and beautifully blends a true story and Scripture. She powerfully shares how trauma and hurt can be overcome and healed. Thank you, Jennifer, for writing this book, which captures the heart and motivates the soul!

KURT SAUDER, Retreat Leader, Executive Director and Co-founder of FurtherStillMinistries.org; Louisville, Kentucky

The real-life story that Jennifer Lynn Heck conveys in her book is riveting! As you read each page of *Walking Victoriously Through a Fiery Furnace,* you will feel like you are there with the characters and experiencing the hurt and pain right along with Victoria Grace. You won't want to put this book down until you finish it and find out how it ends. God is good, all the time!

DEEDREE HALL, Executive Assistant; Louisville, Kentucky

As I read the book, *Walking Victoriously Through a Fiery Furnace,* my first reactions were sadness and anger. Sadness for victims who are abused. Anger for people who take advantage and exploit. Hopefully, the book will spur all of us on toward meaningful action—to be more empathetic with those who are abused and demand justice against those who manipulate. Most of all, to be thankful that one day holy God will reward the righteous and administer justice for the oppressed.

Jennifer Lynn Heck's purpose in writing this book is not to elicit fleeting emotions. Her purpose is to proclaim truth from God's Word and redemption from painful, fiery trials. This book creatively weaves a true story of betrayal and falsehood into the theme of wondrous redemption throughout its inviting, color illustrated pages.

For nearly 30 years, I have known Jennifer, watched her persevere through many faith trials, and been encouraged in my own faith through her tenacious trust in God and her joyful spirit. She has a genuine desire to both live and share the unchanging truth and hope-filled grace of Jesus Christ.

BOB RUSSELL, Speaker and Retreat Leader at BobRussell.org, Retired Senior Pastor at Southeast Christian Church; Louisville, Kentucky

Forgetting the past and looking forward to what lies ahead, I strain to reach the end of the race and receive the prize for which God is calling us up to heaven because of what Christ Jesus did for us.

Philippians 3:13-14, TLB

Made in the USA
Middletown, DE
03 March 2023